D0056978

Advance Praise for *Corporate Boards That Create Value*

"In *Corporate Boards That Create Value*, Carver and Oliver offer totally new insights into an old topic. This rare and remarkable book provides a logical framework for governing in an efficient, accountable manner. The authors' easily understood and brilliantly explained methodology shows how directors can provide complete accountability to shareholders and also empower the management of the enterprise."

—James Gillies, Ph.D., Professor Emeritus, Schulich School of Business, York University, Toronto, and author of *Boardroom Renaissance: Power, Morality and Performance in the Modern Corporation*

"The message of John Carver's and Caroline Oliver's book is clear—governance is the job of the board. It must be the key focus of the board and under its direction and control. By actively implementing the road map provided by the authors, progressive boards will be able to demonstrate that they are committed to promoting a culture of good corporate governance."

—John Hall, FAICD, CEO, Australian Institute of Company Directors

"Carver and Oliver give us a clear, practical, and effective model for governance. This is a model that enables boards to fully grasp their role as trustees and yet frees management to achieve the 'ends' the ownership wants and deserves. Must reading for board members and executives."

—Jack Lowe, Jr., chair and CEO, TDIndustries (top ten in *Fortune*'s 100 Best Companies to Work for in America, 1997 through 2002), Dallas

"*Corporate Boards That Create Value* is a veritable tour de force in the area of corporate governance, a major breakthrough in board leadership. In my opinion, the title Chief Governance Officer and the special illumination of the role and responsibility of those who would serve in that position are the greatest furtherance of servant leadership since Robert K. Greenleaf wrote the original essay, 'The Servant as Leader.'"

—Jim Tatum, CEO, Tatum Motor Company, community college leadership consultant, and former chairman of the R. K. Greenleaf Center for Servant Leadership

"Carver and Oliver provide a unique and innovative model for corporate governance. What's even more remarkable is that the structure of the model allows corporate governance policy to be crafted to tackle the real-life, day-to-day issues facing both boards and management. In so doing, the model provides all stakeholders the comfort of knowing that a rationally structured approach exists for addressing corporate governance and, thereby, fiduciary responsibilities."

—Christine Jacobs, chairman and CEO, Theragenics Corporation
 (Forbes' America's 200 Best Small Companies, 2001), Duluth, Georgia

"Carver and Oliver will challenge your most fundamental beliefs about corporate governance—a true breakthrough in thinking. Investors, directors, and executives should heed their message."

—Dana R. Hermanson, C.P.A., Ph.D., director of research, Corporate
 Governance Center, Kennesaw State University, Kennesaw, Georgia

Corporate Boards That Create Value

John Carver

Caroline Oliver

Foreword by Sir Adrian Cadbury

Corporate Boards That Create Value

Governing Company Performance from the Boardroom

JOSSEY-BASS
A Wiley Company
San Francisco

Published by

JOSSEY-BASS
A Wiley Company
989 Market Street
San Francisco, CA 94103-1741

www.josseybass.com

Copyright © 2002 by John Wiley & Sons, Inc.

Jossey-Bass is a registered trademark of John Wiley & Sons, Inc.

No part of this publication may be reproduced, stored in a retrieval system, or transmitted
in any form or by any means, electronic, mechanical, photocopying, recording, scanning,
or otherwise, except as permitted under Sections 107 or 108 of the 1976 United States
Copyright Act, without either the prior written permission of the Publisher or authorization
through payment of the appropriate per-copy fee to the Copyright Clearance Center,
222 Rosewood Drive, Danvers, MA 01923, (978) 750-8400, fax (978) 750-4744. Requests
to the Publisher for permission should be addressed to the Permissions Department,
John Wiley & Sons, Inc., 605 Third Avenue, New York, NY 10158-0012, (212) 850-6011,
fax (212) 850-6008, e-mail: permreq@wiley.com.

Policy Governance is a registered service mark of John Carver.

Policy samples and monitoring report adapted from materials copyright John Carver and
Miriam Carver.

All drawings copyright John Carver.

Jossey-Bass books and products are available through most bookstores. To contact
Jossey-Bass directly, call (888) 378-2537, fax to (800) 605-2665, or visit our website
at www.josseybass.com.

Substantial discounts on bulk quantities of Jossey-Bass books are available to corporations,
professional associations, and other organizations. For details and discount information,
contact the special sales department at Jossey-Bass.

We at Jossey-Bass strive to use the most environmentally sensitive paper stocks available
to us. Our publications are printed on acid-free recycled stock whenever possible, and our
paper always meets or exceeds minimum GPO and EPA requirements.

Jossey-Bass also publishes its books in a variety of electronic formats. Some content that
appears in print may not be available in electronic books.

Library of Congress Cataloging-in-Publication Data

Carver, John.
   Corporate boards that create value : governing company performance from the
boardroom / John Carver, Caroline Oliver ; foreword by Adrian Cadbury.—1st ed.
      p. cm.— (The Jossey-Bass business & management series)
   Includes bibliographical references and index.
   ISBN 0-7879-6114-0 (alk. paper)
   1. Boards of directors. 2. Corporations—Valuation. I. Oliver, Caroline, 1953–
II. Title. III. Series.
HD2745 .C3722 2002
658.4'22—dc21
                                                                        2002006581

FIRST EDITION
HB Printing   10 9 8 7 6 5 4 3 2 1

The Jossey-Bass

Business & Management Series

Contents

A Few Words About Enron

As this book goes to press, the Enron debacle is receiving overwhelming public as well as corporate and market attention. The governance of Enron illustrates some of the shortcomings of corporate governance to which this book is addressed. But the practices of Enron were not so different from countless other corporations; "there but for the grace of God" can surely be heard in many boardrooms. The most telling commentary on corporate governance, however, comes not from Enron but from *response* to the Enron story.

Massive opprobrium has fallen on top executives, Arthur Andersen, and the audit committee. Comments on the culpability of the board have been scattered and very few. We do not excuse the foregoing actors. But executives are under control of the board; audit committees are organs of the board; auditors, though technically chosen by shareholders, are selected *de facto* by the board. If accountability is to mean more than window dressing, then failure by executives, the audit committee, or the auditor is, in fact, a failure of the board.

Yet discourse about board accountability is largely absent from press coverage and, it appears, from most corporate chatter. The body touted to be "ultimately accountable" gets little attention despite its position at the pinnacle of the organizational chart. The silence speaks volumes about how the corporate world, the press, and the public view boards. This is the silence we will address. Attaining governance accountability and integrity must begin with redesigning how everyone conceives of board leadership—most of all the directors themselves.

Foreword

It is a privilege to be invited to write a foreword to a book that should change our thinking about boards. *Corporate Boards That Create Value* has to be read with an open mind, casting aside the accumulation of accepted practice and approaching the whole subject afresh. We have waited long for a book that analyzes the role of boards from first principles. John Carver and Caroline Oliver have now filled this gap and done so with patient lucidity. As they say, "significant advances in governance will come about only from rethinking the very nature of the board job." The rest of us involved in matters of corporate governance have taken boards as we found them, and sought ways of making the board systems, which were already in place, more effective. The resulting focus on governance and the emergence of codes of best practice have seen a measurable improvement in board effectiveness, powered by market forces. A significant advance, however, in the view of Carver and Oliver, demands a new governance model and not simply further refinements to the existing model.

The Policy Governance model fills that bill and thereby makes a fundamental contribution to the cause of better governance. Each element of the new model is firmly based on logic. As a result, all the elements fit together to form a single, coherent governance structure. For the first time, we are being offered a fully integrated and coherent system of governance. The role of the board is to govern on behalf of the owners. The board alone, therefore, determines the ends of the enterprise, its essential purpose. It does so in the light of the expectations of the owners and acting for the owners. How those ends are achieved is the responsibility of management and involves a choice of means. Means are delegated to management, but within bounds carefully set by the board. Deciding which means are not acceptable is a crucial board responsibility because most of the damage to corporate reputations arises from mistaken means. The clearer the board's policy guidance, the greater the freedom of the executive to use his or her ingenuity and skill to deliver agreed results and the greater his or her ability to act quickly, without reference back to the board, always provided that action is within the bounds.

Boards, as we know them, face the problem of where and how to draw the line between direction, which is the task of the board, and management, which is the task of the executive. The temptation is always for direction to seep into management. Running a business is more immediate, more gripping, and more easily grasped than determining the purpose of the business and setting the framework within which the business has to be managed. The consequence is that boards tend to look inward at management rather than outward to the owners and how best to govern on their behalf. Once a board has defined ends and bounded means, it has established an unequivocal basis for the separation of board and management roles.

The Policy Governance model that is thoroughly worked through in this book represents a significant advance in management thinking. Not only is the model logical and integrated, it is also as near a universal theory of governance as we at present have. It appears applicable to most types of governing bodies in most parts of the world. Its universality provides a benchmark against which to measure the quality of existing governance models of all kinds. I accept the authors' warning, based on experience, of the importance of installing the Policy Governance model as a whole and not introducing it in stages or using it to patch an existing system. Nevertheless, the book does point out which elements in the model could be drawn on to bring greater clarity of purpose and of roles to the structure and workings of any board. Even if board members do not currently envisage adopting the model, the thinking that lies behind it is relevant to any group endowed with governance responsibilities.

A move to the Policy Governance model looks straightforward because the logic behind the model is so clear. Precisely because it is driven by logic, it is uncompromising and cannot be bent to fit personalities in the way we usually treat our organizational structures. It requires a disciplined approach, and discipline is uncomfortable, perhaps especially for those of us used to moderately anarchic board procedures. The board has to discipline itself to deal with every issue through policy. This is considerably more demanding than making or agreeing to decisions as they arise and meddling in management from time to time. Thinking is hard work. Directors working under the Policy Governance model have to construct a framework that both gives the CEO a clear remit over the results to be achieved and sets the limits within which those results are to be achieved. The board has both to prescribe and to proscribe, as the authors point out.

Boards that follow the model are clear about their role, and the confusions referred to earlier over the respective provinces of board and management are resolved. To underline the governance role, Carver and Oliver suggest that whoever chairs the board should be called the chief governance officer (CGO). Although it is hard to change traditional titles, this concept is a powerful one, and one whose time has come. The essential point is the stamp that it puts on the role of the board and of those who chair the board. They are there to govern. By referring to the chair as the chief governance officer, that post is firmly differentiated from that of the chief executive officer.

The next challenge is whether the CEO can also be the CGO. The logic of the model seems to me to add weight to the case for the separation of roles. The more precisely the functions of the board and of management are divided, the more logical it becomes for them to have different heads. Indeed it would be an advantage to a CEO to have someone whose role is as distinctly different as the CGO's role is in the new model with whom to share and debate thoughts, ideas, and concerns. A difficulty with the usual split of duties between chairs and chief executives is that there remains enough common ground between the posts for complementarity to slide into competition. In the model, both posts serve the board, and the chair, or CGO, is not the CEO's boss. The CEO has one master, the board, and one responsibility, managing the business in accordance with the policy framework set by the board. Equally, however, if the posts are to be held by the same person, then the clearer role definitions encapsulated in the new model should make it easier for that person to distinguish between them. Knowing which hat the CGO-CEO is wearing at any given time will also be of benefit to both board members and managers.

Clearly chairs, or CGOs, have a leading part to play in ensuring that governance boards work in the way the new model outlines. As Carver and Oliver say, "We believe that the chair's role is one of the most important keys to unlocking the potential of boards, and we are therefore going to give it considerable attention." I strongly support the importance that the model gives to the chair's role. This book stresses that the board must speak with one voice and that the CEO takes directions only from the board as a whole. The board will speak with one voice only as a result of directors' commitment to do so and the skill of the chair. I doubt that what is required of a person to serve well on any type of board or committee is a natural form of behavior. The key task of a chair is to enable the members of a board to work together effectively and to get the best out of them. This is what the servant achieved in the story on which Robert Greenleaf's concept of the *servant-leader* is based. Chairs have a major leadership task. It is they who are responsible for turning a collection of competent individuals into an effective team. The new model is demanding of its chairs, and much will depend on them.

Another field in which the new model scores high is that of appraisal. One of the more difficult tasks facing boards today is accurately appraising their own performance and that of the executives. A Policy Governance board has clear criteria against which to evaluate its own effectiveness. That is, it evaluates itself against its own terms of reference, having already debated what those terms shall be. Similarly, the CEO and the executive team are appraised in terms of the performance of the company. All appraisal is carried out against known and agreed criteria, with the aim of learning from the process.

One of the outcomes of the design of the new model is that it relates governance to ownership and to active ownership at that. Governance is a separate function in its own right and is not a higher level of management. Governance sets the framework within which whatever is being governed can be managed. Good governance does not involve emasculating management. Strong boards deserve strong executives, and strong executives should welcome working with boards that give them a clear remit and operating freedom within known limits.

The object of *Corporate Boards That Create Value* is to assist boards to make the significant advance of which they are capable in the interests of their owners and more broadly of society. My hope is that this book will be widely read, debated, and discussed by those charged with running organizations of all kinds. We should not shy away from examining the theoretical underpinning of the systems and processes whereby we direct and manage our institutions. As John Carver and Caroline Oliver explain, rational governance must be designed from a coherent paradigm. They have now offered us that paradigm.

Knowle, Solihull, West Midlands   SIR ADRIAN CADBURY
May 2002

Sir Adrian Cadbury has been chairman of the Committee on Financial Aspects of Corporate Governance in the United Kingdom ("The Cadbury Report"), a director of the Bank of England, chairman of Cadbury-Schweppes, and the Chancellor of Aston University. He is the author of *The Company Chairman* and an honorary fellow of King's College, Cambridge.

To Miriam and Ian

Introduction

If we do not concern ourselves with how we can
rule organizations, the organizations will rule us.
                                        —J. Keith Louden[1]

Whether driven by increasing understanding that governance is not simply management writ large, by taunts of "where was the board?" or simply by directors wanting to do a better job, the scene in corporate boardrooms today is encouragingly different from what it was just a few years ago. We believe it can be even better.

This book is about the job of corporate governance. The word governance has several definitions, but in this book it means simply the role of the board of directors. As we proceed, we offer definitions of the nature and proper value of this role and then follow that discussion with implications for everyday corporate life. Consequently, this book is both conceptual and practical.

Calls for boards to exercise their authority over management are increasing. This book explains how boards can assume the full potential of that authority, gaining strength and autonomy without sacrificing management potency. The challenge for strong boards is not so much to tolerate strong management as to *demand* it. Greater board assertiveness, already a fast-developing reality, must be shaped so as to produce powerful management, not feeble management. A coherent and practical concept of governance is needed that drives the changing board-management partnership to function at its best.

What we wish to contribute is an operating system to meet this need—the Policy Governance model. We believe this model offers the coherent and practical concepts required. As a framework, it provides a way for the board to look at corporate issues, separating its role from that of management, delegating powerfully, yet retaining its own accountability. We address, first, the governance mind-set, or—more accurately—the organizing principles of that mind-set, then a process that supports and guides it, and finally the practical documents that capture and codify it. So although we seek to affect the way directors *think*, we also demonstrate how new thinking can enable boards to *act* with a more precise balance of authority retained and authority delegated away.

The Readers of This Book

This book is written, first, for directors who despite recent advances continue to search for insights, new ideas, and even helpful theory. We do not mean to devalue the practical. Far from it. Our goal is to offer practical solutions built on an increasingly coherent framework for corporate governance as a function in its own right. To put a finer point on it, this book is written for those directors who search for a coherent, underlying framework for the board job— practical guidance, to be sure, but practice founded in a carefully constructed set of ideas about the nature of the board job itself.

We also write for people who consign their wealth to the care of corporate directors as well as for those who work for them and with them and those who regulate them. For all involved in governance, be they directors, investors, executives, consultants, academics, or regulators, we offer a way to view, support, and evaluate the stewardship of boards. We ask those of our readers who are not directors to understand that our intention in having the book speak directly to directors is to serve rather than exclude the interests of all readers.

Laying the Foundations

Before demonstrating the concrete application of the Policy Governance model, we ask the reader to consider a number of ideas— some familiar and some not, some easily accepted and some not.

These ideas create the foundation, the context, from which the practical application logically flows. Readers will have varied responses to these ideas, as people do with any new way to organize any work. Some directors will find nothing new here but a codification of their own beliefs. Some directors will find only ideas with which they are instantly comfortable. Others will find the ideas strange, at least initially.

Our goal has been to minimize barriers to understanding, but we cannot completely avoid one particular hurdle: specialized language. Much as we want to minimize jargon in a jargon-filled world, we find that new concepts and new ways to organize old wisdom often require new tags to distinguish them from old ideas or more familiar ways. New terms as well as common terms that we are using in particular ways are defined in the glossary in Appendix A.

Explaining how and why the Policy Governance model works appears to us to be a responsibility as large as the potential rewards it offers of corporate transparency, clarity, role definition, and accountability. We know from many years' experience in working with boards that the substantial changes this book proposes produce significant improvement in directors' perception of their effectiveness. We also know that highly effective governance is impossible unless the conceptual foundations are fully laid.

Governance, Not Management

Underlying this book is the assumption that governing a company and managing it are different activities requiring different job designs. We maintain that governance is best seen as existing *outside* the phenomenon of management and *inside* the phenomenon of ownership. Governance operates at a level that transcends current issues and specific company traditions and elevates people to a higher conceptual plane, one from which accountability can be seen more clearly. Governance requires and engenders a passion for leadership, leadership that is not just over others but on others' behalf.

This book is not about merely adding more "best practices." Practices stem from individuals' views of the world. Whatever your view of the board's accountability, you might profitably spend time learning improved methods, protocols, and techniques to better fulfill that view of the job. But better practices rarely change the view itself, much as word processors did not evolve through efforts to improve typewriters. Recent years have seen an explosion of interest in best practices, and we hope that interest continues. But our contribution is to question and recommend change in the view of the job itself. To the extent we are successful, organizations should see a whole new round of best practices—ones built on this new paradigm.

We believe that despite all the increased attention to the topic of governance and the resulting improvements to board structures, processes, and practices, a fundamental deficiency remains. This book sets out to fill that gap by unifying governance concepts and practices in one logical operating system, Policy Governance.

What You Will Learn

As we set out the Policy Governance framework, you will be introduced to some perspectives on governance that will be of interest whether or not your board ultimately decides to use them. To give you a flavor of what is to come, we offer the following propositions:

- Significant advances in governance will occur only when people recognize that governance is not a subcategory or extension of management but a subcategory or extension of ownership. *The nature of board work, then, is not management one step up but ownership one step down.*

- A board must be an active, deciding, independent link in the chain of authority from owners to operators. *Accountable boards, then, are commanders, not advisers.*

- Assertive fulfillment of the board's authority need not yield weak management. *Proper delegation, then, must result in board control and management empowerment simultaneously.*

- As long as governance is CEO-centric or chair-centric, excellence in representing owners will remain beyond reach. *Responsible governance, then, must be board-centric and board controlled.*

- The proper chair is not boss but first among equals as the board's crucial servant-leader, responsible to the board for ensuring that it successfully governs. *Tomorrow's chair, then, is not top management but is best conceived as—and, even better, titled as—chief governance officer (CGO).*

- Leading a group of equals to define and demand successful execution is an entirely different process from leading subordinates in achieving successful execution. *Clear separation of the roles of chair and CEO, then, is critical even when the positions are combined in one person.*

- Transparency with owners and with society is impeded when the board does not make its values explicit and available or allows the management of information or performance to be hidden. *Transparency outside, then, is markedly dependent on transparency inside.*

- Traditional practices, even best practices, though clearly a collection of wisdom, are limited in how much improvement they can offer because they are not derived from a conceptually sound whole. *More mature governance, then, will be designed from a coherent paradigm instead of assembled from parts.*

- Although structure, process, and practice matter, significant advances in governance will come about only from rethinking the very nature of the board job. *Powerful governance, then, will derive from consideration of the value the board should add plus a design of the job rigorous enough to produce that value.*

How This Book Is Organized

We develop the Policy Governance model and its implications for corporate governance sequentially, and therefore this book is designed to be read in the order that it is presented. Chapter One considers the value that boards add now and, from an examination of the source and nature of board authority, suggests a redefinition and elevation of the value that they create. Chapter Two sets out the basics of Policy Governance design, through which boards can deliver that value. Chapters Three, Four, and Five apply the design to the board's process, its relationship with the CEO, and the manner in which it commands company performance. Chapter Six addresses the mechanics of accountability—acquiring and using adequate reports of company performance. Chapter Seven examines what boards can do to make sure that they stay on track. Chapter Eight describes a typical implementation process.

In order to maintain the flow of the book, we have placed a number of important arguments and resources in the appendixes. Appendix A is a glossary of the terms we either introduce or use in unfamiliar ways. Appendix B extends remarks made in the text concerning the term *chief governance officer* as a clarification of the chair's role. Appendix C argues against combining the chair and CEO jobs in one person, even though the Policy Governance model requires only that the roles be kept separate whether or not combined in one person. Appendix D addresses the inclusion on boards of inside (nonexecutive) directors. Appendix E provides a set of sample policies that includes and supplements examples provided in the main text. Appendix F gives an example of a policy monitoring report.

Our Focus

A sole focus on a framework for governance is a narrow one, yet in a sense it is the broadest focus of all. For the aim of the framework is to provide a way of conceiving everything about the upper reaches of any corporation—all the various levels of decisions, types of decisions, accountabilities, job designs, and authorities. This is a simple book about a very complex subject, seeking to provide a rational framework on which all governance decisions may be hung, a road map to proper use of directors' talent, sense of responsibility, and foresight.

We do not address the content of the many decisions that boards face. By content, we mean the bodies of knowledge needed to make wise decisions about specific endeavors, such as mergers, acquisitions, stock option plans, public offerings, entering new markets, and a host of other challenges. Instead, we address the underlying issues of what a board is for, how it can separate its role in decision making from management's role, how it can delegate powerfully yet not let its own responsibility slip away, how it can be more activist without weakening management, how it can distinguish between information needed to govern and information needed to manage, and how it can be in control without meddling.

We believe a more coherent paradigm than has previously existed for corporate governance has the power to clarify and enrich much of the ongoing conversation about leadership, accountability, and policymaking as well as to support and inspire increasingly effective practices. It is to these ends that this book is written.

Atlanta, Georgia   JOHN CARVER
Oakville, Ontario   CAROLINE OLIVER
May 2002

Corporate Boards That Create Value

Chapter One

The Value of Boards

If legitimacy is to be restored to the system, the chain
of accountability must be made more effective.
—*David S. R. Leighton and Donald H. Thain*[1]

In This Chapter

- The importance of corporate governance
- The value that boards create

Corporate governance, once overlooked, is now center stage.
There is widespread agreement that corporate boards are vital to
total company leadership and to the role of corporations in society.
Many participants in and observers of the corporate scene believe
that corporate governance is of real value in improving company
performance and investors' perceptions.

This growing sense of the fundamental importance of good governance is also reflected in the explosion of expectations being placed
on boards. These expectations come in the form of advisory guidelines, principles, and codes of practice, along with prescriptive statutes
and regulations laid down by governments and their agencies, such as
the U.S. Securities Exchange Commission. There are now more than
sixty corporate governance codes issued by stock exchanges and other
authoritative groups from around the world, in addition to the
bewildering array of regional, national, and international statutes.

The spotlight has also been intensified by the recent spate of books on governance; by media reports of corporate news, including high-profile disasters, that discuss board action and inaction; and by frequent news of shareholder activism.

All this attention has spurred many boards to make significant improvements. Among these improvements are greater transparency, more independence from management, changes in audit committee composition, and separation of the board chair role and the CEO role. The subject of corporate governance has been opened up as never before, but we make the case in this book that there is yet another, more advanced level of excellence available.

Incidentally, in this book we use the words *company* and *corporation* interchangeably. We reserve the word *business* to mean not an organization but a type of activity in which a company may be engaged.

What Is the Value That Boards Create?

Our title, *Corporate Boards That Create Value*, begs a big question. Most people agree that in today's challenging marketplace no part of any corporation can be merely ceremonial. In fact, much corporate governance discussion during the past two decades has implored boards to *add value*. But what value is that to be? We start to answer that question by looking at the responses that could be derived from current board practices:

Expert advice. Directors act as a group of expert advisers to management. They bring skills, knowledge, and experience in relevant management specialties or management in general. Sometimes advice comes from the board as a whole, but often it comes from individual directors, leaving the position of the board as a *group* unclear. Sometimes the board is proactive in this advisory role; it suggests or probes for subjects on which its advice should be solicited. Sometimes it acts more as a sounding board to which managers can turn when and if they choose. A closely related contribution that the board may make is developing managers.

Safeguards. The board provides security, particularly for investors, through checking that all is well in the company and ensuring proper disclosure of information. To do this, the board typically requires management to bring its major plans and intentions for board approval and to subsequently update the board with progress reports. When the board sees something it doesn't like, it acts as a circuit breaker, either setting existing management back on track or putting new management in place.

Useful connections. Directors' positions and contacts in other settings are used to benefit the company on whose board they sit, in terms of finance, public relations, and potential customers.

These kinds of contributions are not insignificant, and they are being improved upon all the time as boards are introduced to additional best practice codes and advice. This book, however, makes the case that the responsibility and value creation potential of boards goes further. Our thesis is that boards can create much greater value than they do today. However, to understand how this can be done, the value boards contribute and the design of the job that creates that value must be reexamined and reframed. The rest of this chapter will begin this reexamination and reframing, making the case, first, for a new and more ambitious definition of the value boards should create and, second, for a board job redesigned, that is, reengineered, from the ground up with the purpose of creating that value.

Why Do Boards Exist?

To establish a definition of the value of boards requires us to start at the very beginning. So our earlier question—what is the value that boards create?—must be revised too. Instead, we need to ask, where does the board's authority come from, what is the reason for that authority, and what is the nature of that authority? In other words, why do boards exist?

The Source of Board Authority

Companies' *owners* are the source of board authority, those on whose behalf it does its job. Most boards in most parts of the world consider shareholders their company's owners, but there are exceptions. For example, in some countries the state has legislated that employees are owners. Moreover, there are many who argue that limiting the concept of ownership to shareholders is to accept far too narrow a definition. Some argue[2] that boards in today's global and interdependent world, whatever their legal situation, are morally obliged to include many other groups of *stakeholders* as owners—groups such as employees, customers, creditors, suppliers, and the community at large. The core of their argument is that these stakeholders have an investment in the company, albeit not one of equity, and that these nonequity investments should also count as an ownership interest.

The picture is further complicated by the fact that shareholders range from the small individual investor to the large institutional investor. They range from those with little or no power to those who, because of the size of their holdings, have a controlling interest. They range from those who vote only by assigning proxies to those who turn up at every annual general meeting. Further, subject to the current ownership's agreement, boards have the power to create different classes of ownership (differentiating, for example, between owners of common and preferred stock) with different voting rights and therefore different levels of power within the overall ownership.

The board's role as arbiter among various interests is certainly more important today than ever before. Legal owners are, of course, the only ones who have the power to overrule the board. But with the legal ownership's consent, the board can affect the composition of investors to whom the company will be attractive, thereby exercising a proactive role in deciding who the owners will be.[3] All we need to recognize for the purposes of this discussion is that owners, however they are defined, are the source of the board's authority.

The Reason for Board Authority

Incorporation gives a company a distinct legal identity separate from the people who own and operate it. This separation, the extent of which varies across the world's jurisdictions, provides protection from risk for owners and freedom to act for operators. The extent to which public policy should control matters such as company size, power, political involvement, and impact on the environment will likely always be the subject of debate. Although boards have no authority over the legal framework in which they operate, they do have enormous power in bridging the gap between the company's owners and operators.

Because owners are the source of a company's authority, it follows that the need for a governing board arises only when the owners are too numerous to direct and control the company themselves. Therefore, the notion of board authority as a distinct kind of authority occurs only when there is a gap between the ownership of assets and the management of those assets. That is, this gap between the ownership of assets and the management of those assets has led to the notion of a distinct kind of authority—board authority. The board's position is, therefore, to act as the link between owners and management, directing and controlling the company on the owners' behalf. Put another way, the reason owners grant such authority is to enable the board to act as the ownership in microcosm.

The Nature of Board Authority

An examination of the nature of board authority must start, then, with the board's position in the sequence of legitimate corporate authority. A proper chain of accountability guarantees *legitimacy*, a legitimacy that is essential for corporate governance. How the board is thus situated has far-reaching implications for the design and duties of governance.

Highest Authority. In any company the board is at the top in the chain of accountability and therefore at the top of the chain of command. The phrase *chain of command*, with its hierarchical con-notations, is not used casually here. We use it to describe a rank of authority, not a desirable management style. We use it to indicate the fact that authority is the power to command (to direct and con-trol) and passes sequentially from the source of authority to the out-ermost reaches of its expression.

The accountability chain is weakened when the board fails to recognize that it has the *obligation*, not just the authority, to com-mand. As the owners' representative, the board has no right *not* to exercise those owners' rightful prerogatives. The board has no responsible alternative but to be authoritative in its role, lest own-ers lose their voice.

Initial Authority. The board cannot abdicate its prerogatives. That means it cannot allow them to be defined or assumed by the CEO or by any of the company's employees or by any sub-component of the board, including the chair. These assertions are inescapable—all authority exercised in the company flows initially from the board, even if by default. As the supreme authority (after the owners), the board must be in full control of its own job before presuming to control anything else. This requires that the board as a group be responsible for its actions, its omissions, its agendas, the delegations it makes, and the corporate values it imposes.

Management doesn't work directly for owners; only the board does. Therefore the board makes demands on management perfor-mance from an independent position. This means that the board is authoritative, not advisory. It also means the board has a specific, definable job and is not just the overseer of someone else's job. Because the board is the sole source of on-site corporate authority, no person or groups of persons (except owners) can have any authority whatsoever unless the board grants that authority. Proper governance, therefore, must be proactive in distributing authority, establishing expectations about the proper use of that authority, and then demanding performance. In this way the board is trans-formed from today's frequently reactive *final* authority into the highest and *initial* authority.

Accountable Authority. Because the board is the overall authority in a company, it is accountable to owners for its own performance and that of the company. And because no one has any authority unless the board has granted it, the board has control over how well all authority is exercised. Consequently, the board cannot blame poor board performance on its chair, on the chief executive, or on any of its committees. Poor chair performance indicates a poor board. Poor chief executive performance indicates a poor board. Poor audit, executive, or compensation committee performances indicate a poor board. And of course poor company performance indicates a poor board. Accountability is a harsh concept indeed. But it is an inescapable element in any legitimate system of authority.

Group Authority. The board possesses authority only as a group. Individual directors, including the chair, have no authority unless specifically given it by the group. In later chapters we examine how a group can perform this *first cause* role. For now we simply want to underline the principle that board authority is group authority.

Empowering Authority. One of the central challenges for boards is how to *command* in such a way that management is optimally empowered and challenged at the same time. Good governance must integrate a compelling approach to delegation—one that is rigorous in safeguarding the board's own accountability yet as freeing and empowering of others as it can responsibly be. When the board underplays its role, owners are cheated in that their only legitimate and authoritative representative has a weak voice. When a board overplays its role, owners are cheated in that their only legitimate and authoritative representative does not know how to get the most out of management.

The Value Boards Should Create

The logical conclusion from this examination of universal principles of governance (summarized in Exhibit 1.1) is simply this: a board is a body accountable to the owners as a whole that operates

Exhibit 1.1. Universal Principles of Accountable Governance.

- The board governs on behalf of all owners.
- The board is the highest authority, under owners, in the company.
- The board is the initial authority in the company.
- The board is accountable for everything about the company.
- All authority and accountability is vested in the board as a group.
- Governance roles and executive roles have different purposes.
- Delegation should be maximized, short of risking the board's fulfillment of its accountability.
- Assessing board performance requires evaluation of both governance and management.

as the highest, initial authority in a company, and therefore the value it creates is *translating owners' wishes into company performance*.

Looking Back, Moving Forward

In this chapter, from a consideration of the fundamental reasons boards exist, we proposed a definition of the value that boards should create: *translating owners' wishes into company performance*. This sounds like a very tall if not impossible order for a small group of part-time people. Yet this is the responsibility that belongs uniquely to boards and that beyond all other grounds justifies their existence. How boards can deliver on that responsibility is a matter of job design—a challenge to which the rest of this book is devoted.

Chapter Two

Designing the Board's Job

At this point in history, existing mechanisms for
governing corporations are no longer adequate.
The scale, complexity, importance, and risks of
corporate activity have overrun our institutions.
—*Ada Demb and F.-Friedrich Neubauer*[1]

In This Chapter

- Why policy is the board's most essential tool
- What governing through policy looks like
- How policy levels allow delegation of real authority
- Why ends and means require different methods of control

In the previous chapter we set out the source and nature of the
board's authority, the fundamental basis for a new governance
design. In this chapter we explain how the framework provided by
the Policy Governance model enables boards to meet the challenge
of translating the wishes of company owners into company performance. Our assertion is that boards that adopt this framework will
be far better equipped to provide accountable and effective leadership than are boards that follow conventional practice.

Better Governance by Design

In offering a universal model for corporate governance, we recognize
that companies' traditions, histories, arrangements, and structures
will and must vary considerably. But we contend categorically that

there are underlying truths common to all bodies that on behalf of a wider group wield authority over organizations.

Before describing the Policy Governance framework in detail, this section highlights several key features that make this model uniquely suited to the job of governance. The Policy Governance model is a total system that

Derives from the purpose and nature of board authority. The model is applicable to all boards because its point of departure is the generic purpose and nature of board authority rather than structures and processes that are current in general practice or are peculiar to a specific industry. Starting from underlying basics produces governance principles that typically, in our experience, make common sense to directors, executives, and others. The resulting shared perception of the board's purpose and nature yields a foundation for designing governance so that the board can handle real-world, specific issues from a coherent and powerful perspective.

Is custom-made for the governing job. The nature of governance and its requirements in terms of processes, structures and skills are not the same as those of management. The model has borrowed from and is compatible with the work of management but was invented deliberately for the work of governance.

Encompasses the whole job. Governance must be designed to encompass the board's accountability for every aspect of the company. However, it must also be designed so that the board's reach does not exceed its grasp. The model enables a board to embrace yet not become entangled in the entire company. The model does not tell directors the content of their decisions, but it does provide a framework within which they can make effective decisions about everything in and under their authority.

Clarifies who does what. Any lack of clarity in the respective roles of the three most powerful components of company life—owners, directors, and managers—jeopardizes effectiveness. The model defines all the various roles so they are consistent with a common set of governance principles, rather than allowing role definition to be dictated by immediate necessities and current personalities.

Provides predictable results with the fewest possible working parts. Because the job of the board requires busy directors to exercise reliable control over everything, a governance model should make their task as simple as possible. The Policy Governance model identifies a comprehensive set of *tools* with which the board can cut through corporate complexity, using a precision approach to the challenge at hand rather than just adding more things for directors to do.

Reinventing Policy

Policy Governance works through policies. Nothing new here. However, we are not talking about just any policies. When we say *policy* we mean something very different from the familiar kinds of policy and procedures found in most companies. The policy that enables precision company governance follows certain principles in both its subject matter and in its composition, or architecture. It is not the kind of policy that sits on the shelf during or between board meetings or is produced for the sake of demonstrating good form. It is not the traditional expression of intentions and hopes that is forgotten almost as soon as it is written. We are talking about policy that is specifically created, structured, and engineered for the board's job and that actively *embraces* the company's every move. From this point on, whenever we use the word *policy*, we mean only the kind of policy defined in the Policy Governance model and not policy as traditionally described or used.

The Importance of Written Policies

The board needs to be able to convey its decisions on behalf of owners to management and to hold itself accountable to owners for those decisions. Written policies are a tool for conveying the board's decisions to all in a consistent and enduring manner. Unless the board agrees on a written, and therefore explicit, statement of its will, only those who were in the boardroom when that will was stated *and* who have long and totally accurate memories know what a board has said. Everyone else lacks that knowledge.

The decisions, including definitions of roles and relationships (for roles and relationships are also the results of decisions), of the players in corporate governance should be clearly reflected in appropriate documents. They should be available to every relevant party in succinct, easily retrievable, centralized form. As we will illustrate shortly, we do not mean large documents. We do not mean the company should tie itself up in procedures or detailed prescriptions. The board should be rigorous in controlling not all it can, only all it must.

The Twin Problems of Conventional Policy Writing

But even though the written word is far more accurate than the remembered spoken word, two significant problems remain. First, there is the problem of meaning. It may be clear what the board has said, but it may not be so clear what the board *means*. Words are always open to interpretation, so any relationship that relies on words must deal with the inaccuracy of communication.

Second, the board has the problem of choosing what to put into policy and what not to put into policy. In companies, as in life, people's values and perspectives control everything, whether or not they appear in the company handbook. Thus it follows that if the board could identify all its values and perspectives about everything relevant to the company and state them as policy, it could control the whole company. The problem of course is that the sheer number of policies necessary would be impossible even to consider.

Recognizing Decisions Within Decisions

Policy Governance uses a simple concept to solve the twin problems of meaning and infinite policy choice. This concept allows the board to clarify its intent in a manner that embraces all possible actions and aspects of company life. It gives the board the ability to control uncountable single decisions through a few carefully expressed policies.

The concept starts from a recognition that decisions are not all equal in their scope—decisions come in sizes. This fact can be used to circumscribe meaning to a greater or lesser extent and, as it turns out, to control the amount of decision making that is delegated. Simply put, directors can keep out of the details if they make the broad decisions and entrust the smaller decisions within those broad decisions to others. Using the concept of *decisions-within-decisions*, the board can control everything by making its decisions in a cascading sequence of descending *breadths* or *levels*, stopping at the level where the board is willing to allow a delegatee to use *any reasonable interpretation* of its words. The board's job is then distinguished from management's job not by topic (for example, strategy, human resources, or risk), but *by levels within topics*.

By *delegatee*, we mean any among the number of persons to whom the board delegates. Although the CEO is usually foremost among the delegatees in sheer volume of delegation, the same principles will apply as the board delegates to its chair and its committees. At this stage of our discussion, we consider them all simply delegatees.

A useful device for understanding the *decisions-within-decisions* concept of Policy Governance more fully is to think of it as a set of nested bowls (Figure 2.1). The bowls are neatly stacked one within the other, from largest to the smallest. The largest bowl constrains all the smaller bowls, and each of the bowls, except the largest, is constrained by a slightly larger bowl. Viewed as decisions, the larger bowls represent the broader decisions, and the smaller bowls represent the narrower range of decisions that may be made through a *reasonable interpretation* of the decisions symbolized by the larger bowls.

For an illustration of this concept in practice, consider a board policy that says management should avoid a "hostile working environment." However, just what is meant by *hostile* or, for that matter,

Figure 2.1. Decisions as a Nested Set.

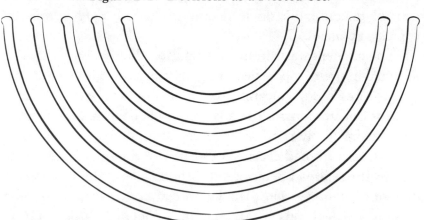

Smaller bowls fit within larger bowls as smaller issues fit within larger ones. Like a set of real bowls, the entire set can be controlled through the direct control of only the outermost, most inclusive bowl.

by *working environment?* On the one hand, the *board* might further define these terms. In this case, it is easy to conceive of the more detailed descriptions as a smaller bowl inside the larger one of "hostile working environment." On the other hand, the board might choose not to go into the extra level of detail. In this case, *management* would have to define "hostile working environment" further, because *achieving* any reasonable interpretation of what the board said at the broad level requires *making* such an interpretation. This is true whether or not the governance system explicitly recognizes it. In Policy Governance, this phenomenon is not only explicitly recognized but harnessed to empower both the board and management.

Determining Decision Sizes

Because decisions come in all sizes, boards need to distinguish one size from another. It is vital that the board always starts at the broadest decision level. The only surefire way of making certain that the board leaves nothing important out and says no more than it needs to say is to make *every* decision at the broadest, most encompassing level first before moving to the next, narrower level. That is, if board decision making begins with any bowl other than the largest one, the board cannot ensure that the company is really under its control, for a subordinate may be making larger decisions than the board. And the only way the board can choose the level of decisions that it will not worry about controlling directly is by first making the broader decisions that control the range of all possible narrower decisions.

Whether to enter the market for widgets is one size of decision. Whether to enter the subsidiary market for type A widgets versus the subsidiary market for type B widgets, or both, is a smaller decision that fits within the first one. And one can easily conceive of yet smaller decisions limited by the second market decision. For example, having decided to market type B widgets, one might confront a decision whether to produce the more expensive but longer lasting B1 widget or the less expensive but shorter lived B2 sort.

That reasoning is simple enough but applies only to one line of thought. For example, it would be impossible to place a decision between a defined benefit pension plan and a defined contribution pension plan into the same set of bowls that contains a decision between A and B widgets. In other words, the bowl analogy works only with a single line of branching decisions, not with dissimilar decisions. Yet, clearly, corporate life includes a vast number of decisions of different sizes and types.

We will turn to a discussion of types (rather than sizes) of decisions in a moment. But, first, we explore the nested bowls concept a bit further as it relates to the board's being totally accountable yet delegating the vast majority of responsibility for operational management.

Allowing for Reasonable Interpretation

As shown previously, conceiving of the board's words as signifying ranges of interpretation establishes a basic framework for delegation from one level of authority to the next lower one, a framework that can be thought of as a nested set. If a superior makes a "large bowl decision," the subordinate can be given the right to make "small bowl decisions" as long as the nesting is maintained, that is, as long as the subordinate makes decisions that can reasonably be said to be within the larger ones. The fact that a range of reasonable interpretations exists means that the subordinate is granted real authority, the right to make real decisions, but always within the range. The size of the range is set by the level of description at which the superior chooses to stop and determines the extent of delegated authority.

One might contend that there is a workable alternative to delegating authority to make any reasonable interpretation to management. Management can make its interpretations then present them to the board for sanction. With this approach the board need not delegate to management the authority to interpret the board's words. Remember, however, that there are many such interpretations going on all the time in a company and, beyond that, those interpretations are continually being remade due to shifting circumstances. Consequently, this alternative of continually seeking board approval hobbles management, as it struggles with the constant chore of getting an uncountable number of decisions expeditiously made. It also overwhelms the board with managerial decisions on a level at which the board would prefer not to be involved. The Policy Governance model requires the board to choose its words carefully, then to grant management the right to interpret them, demanding that management's smaller bowl decisions always be within the board's decisions.

When someone orders a plain omelet in a restaurant, she implies that the cook can use any reasonable interpretation of her order. She has specified that it must lack fillings, but she hasn't specified the amount of salt, water, or milk to be used. She has left that to the cook's reasonable interpretation of the words *plain omelet*. When someone buys a ticket at a train station, he specifies his destination and the mode and timing of transport, but he leaves the selection of fuel grades and drivers to others. Although the concept of *reasonableness* may itself seem to be plagued by vagueness, it is a standard used quite successfully in law and regularly in everyday life.

The board must accept that what it *means* to say will be of no effect unless it actually says it—that is, unless it advances into the next smaller bowl and in doing so selects one interpretation out of the range of interpretations available in the broader level. However, there will always be a smaller bowl inside that one as well, and another inside that and so on and on. The progression from largest bowl to smallest may not be infinite, but it is surely a long way down to the bowls that address the most trivial possible decisions. The board would massively complicate its own task if it were to make all further, smaller decisions. So the board faces an impossible situation unless at some point it authorizes someone besides itself to make an interpretation of its words (Figure 2.2).

Returning to our restaurant diner illustration, if her plain omelet is made with too much salt, she will not be able to claim

Figure 2.2. Retained and Delegated Authority.

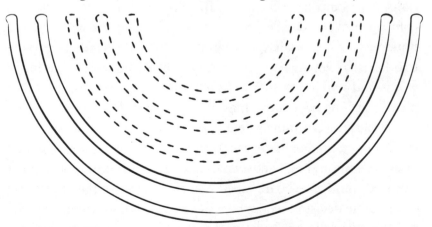

Direct control of the outer bowls in a nested set allows indirect control of the inner bowls. A board might decide to have direct (hands-on) control over the very largest issues (the solid-line bowls) but indirect (hands-off) control of smaller issues (the dotted-line bowls).

that the cook has ignored her salt instructions inasmuch as she did not give such instructions. However, she will certainly be within her rights to return the dish on the basis that the cook has used an unreasonable interpretation of the words *plain omelet*. Yet even after such an experience, she will be unlikely to abandon the any reasonable interpretation rule, for if she decides never to eat in a restaurant unless the cook agrees to be directly supervised by her, chances are she will not be dining out too often.

In like manner the board must accept that it cannot directly supervise a delegatee's every move and neither can it fault the delegatee's interpretation unless a majority of directors find that interpretation unreasonable. In our experience with boards that use the Policy Governance model, disputes between the board and its delegatees over whether an interpretation was reasonable are extremely rare.

Building Precise and Concise Policies

Policy Governance requires the board to be disciplined in using words carefully to convey meaning at an appropriate breadth, thereby leaving to others the exact amount of decision-making range the board intends. Using this approach the board builds a compendium of broad decisions, formatted as policies, within which it judges that it can safely and explicitly leave the smaller decisions to others. In exchange for the trouble of being precise in crafting its words and making occasional amendments to its decisions, the board reaps the benefit of a massive amount of safe delegation.

Because it contains a few large issues and not uncountable smaller ones, the board's master document of policies is surprisingly brief. The tug and pull between under- and overcontrol is avoided. On one hand the board does not engage in rubber-stamping, because the decision sequence moves from board to management, not the other way around. On the other hand the board does not engage in micromanagement, because engagement in details is not needed to gain control. (Exhibit 2.1 summarizes the characteristics offered by the policy design of the Policy Governance model.)

Leading from the Front

An essential benefit of this method of delegating authority is that it enables the board, using a rational process of consideration and discussion, to define ahead of time what it wants. Although reactive adjustments may certainly be made when needed, the board's way of life does not revolve around reactions to current circumstances or to subordinates' agendas. The independence of judgment and proactivity in leadership this implies is crucial to improved governance.

The need for board proactivity arises because the board is the initial authority and must form an active link in the chain of command. The board that fails to be in the front of the parade makes a

Exhibit 2.1. Policy Design Distinctions of Policy Governance.

1. **Policies control everything**—embracing all of governance and management.
2. **Policies are written**—together they form the paramount board document except for incorporation documents and bylaws.
3. **Policies come in sizes**—controlling the broadest range of decisions and such narrower ones as the board chooses.
4. **Policies are created in size sequence**—progressing from the broadest level toward the narrowest, stopping where any reasonable interpretation of the words would be acceptable.
5. **Policies are accurate and concise**—expressing the board's meaning clearly, briefly, and without repetition.
6. **Policies are assembled in categories tailored for governing**—separating ends from management's means and from the board's means.
7. **Policies are in regular use**—forming an immediately available and frequently referenced document relevant to governance and management, updated as necessary.
8. **Policies are generated by the board**—not by management for board approval.
9. **Policies are current**—displaying the accumulation of board values in effect at any given time rather than a sequentially historical record as minutes do.
10. **Policies are centrally available**—not scattered through many locations and types of documents.

charade out of responsible governance and owner-representative accountability. It is impossible for a board to delegate authority it does not know it has or, as is more frequently the case, has never embraced as its own to begin with.

The board's responsibility does not consist of waiting for management to do, say, or propose something. In fact, we maintain that no element of the board's job is determined by management. This is not to say there is no interaction, for there is a great deal. It is also not to say that the board cannot learn from and even be inspired by management. It is only to say that in the proper sequence of things, management's job is determined by the board, not the board's by management.

Utilizing the Durability of Values

Because Policy Governance policy arises from the board's standing back and asking what its overall values for the company are, it does not tend to be the kind of policy that gets rapidly outdated. For similar reasons, the kind of judgment involved in this policymaking does not typically involve intimate knowledge of the matter at hand but the kind of broad knowledge and experience that equips a thoughtful person to weigh a great many matters and arrive at a wise conclusion.

Separating Ends and Means

We now return to the question of how the board can keep issues of different types in separate nests of bowls. This is another critical piece of the design that enables a board to be powerful in its role yet grants as much authority to other roles as possible. First, it is necessary to separate corporate ends from corporate means.

When we talk of ends, we avoid the words *goals*, *objectives*, and *strategies* because such words are commonly used to refer to both ends and means. We use *ends* to describe what the company is *for* rather than what it *does*.[2] Ends distinguish purpose from path, results from process, and where one is going from how one is going to get there. For example, a company might be in business so that shareholders have a long-term return above the market average. It is definitely not in business for the purpose of having a particular plant, distribution system, or even product—these are means.

We define corporate *means* as any decisions or realities that are not ends—a definition by exclusion. Means include activities, practices, methods, technology, conduct, systems, and a host of operational decision areas as well as decisions about governance. What is important to notice here is that every single corporate issue can be defined either as an ends issue or as a means issue. For the moment, we are not discussing who makes either kind of decision. An issue is an ends issue or a means issue as a result of its nature, not as a result of who makes a decision about it.

Differential Control of Ends and Means

The reason it is important to distinguish ends and means clearly from each other is that in the Policy Governance model, the board that is delegating decisions about ends and means to management must control those decisions differently. Ends are best controlled in an affirmative, prescriptive way, whereas the means of striving toward ends are best controlled in a limiting, proscriptive way. To codify and control its own means, the means of governance, the board may express itself in whatever terms it sees appropriate, but ordinarily that would be positive or prescriptive.

To control ends (what the company is for) in an affirmative and prescriptive way, the board communicates its performance expectations to its delegatees in terms of return, share price in relation to market, or whatever other items in the board's judgment are appropriate benchmarks of corporate success *from the owners' perspective*. To control management's means (what the company does), however, the board does not tell management what to do, but what *not* to do. That is, controlling management's means decisions is done through boundary setting that puts off limits those choices about means that the board would find unacceptable. We explain how this works in Chapter Five.

Policy Categories Based on Ends and Means

To encompass every aspect of a company, boards must make policy in four policy categories. The first two are means categories that address the board's own job. The other two instruct management concerning desired ends and unacceptable means.

First, the board needs policies to control its own behavior—its governance processes and practices. We call this category **Governance Process.** Second, the board needs to set out how it is going to delegate its authority to management and yet remain accountable for the use of that authority. We call this category **Board-Management Delegation.** Third, the board must establish the ends—some form of owner value—justifying the company's existence and defining the central value it adds to the world. We call this category **Ends.** Fourth, the board expresses the limitations or constraints that define the limits of acceptability as management makes means decisions. We call this category **Management Limitations.**

Exhibit 2.2 sets out the policy categories used in the Policy Governance model to cover every single issue that a corporation faces. Each category is explored in more detail in later chapters, including the rationale for the negative language of Management Limitations. The exact titles used for these categories are not important, but the conceptual separation of the categories is. For example, a given board might choose to say Shareholder Value (that is, a specific end) instead of Ends, Executive Constraints instead of Management Limitations, Board Job instead of Governance Process, and Governance-Management Linkage instead of Board-Management Delegation— or any other language of its choosing.

The Policy Circle

The policy circle (Figure 2.3) takes our nested bowls analogy to a new level. The full display of bowls is now divided into four quadrants representing the four categories. Each quadrant contains all the decisions

Exhibit 2.2. Categories of Board Policy.

When the board sets policy that controls the following four categories, even at a very broad level, the board controls the organization because all that governance and management might do, be, cause, or allow is included in these categories.

- **Governance Process:** policies prescribe the board's internal operations, governance methods, accountabilities, and philosophy.
- **Board-Management Delegation:** policies prescribe the board's methods of delegating and monitoring responsibility for management performance.
- **Ends:** policies prescribe what value the company is to produce on owners' behalf, usually some form of shareholder value.
- **Management Limitations:** policies put ethics and prudence boundaries around the company's methods, activities, conduct, and risks.

that are possible in a company in that category, both governance and management decisions. As before, the concentric circles, the larger and smaller bowls, show that in each quadrant there are larger and smaller decisions. Decisions about governance itself are shown in the upper left quadrant (Governance Process). Decisions about connecting governance and management are in the lower left quadrant (Board-Management Delegation). Decisions about corporate ends are in the upper right quadrant (Ends). And decisions about managerial means are in the lower right quadrant (Management Limitations).

The board's policymaking task is to make the largest decisions in each quadrant, leaving smaller decisions to the board's delegatees. Figure 2.4 illustrates a completed policy circle in which the board has filled in the larger reaches of each quadrant, leaving the inner domains to the board chair and CEO—a subject we shall be saying a lot more about later.

Policy Samples

In the following chapters and in Appendix E we give samples of policies that boards might create in each of the policy categories. We want to emphasize that these are merely samples. However, directors will see that many of these policies could easily be adapted to their

Figure 2.3. The Policy Circle.

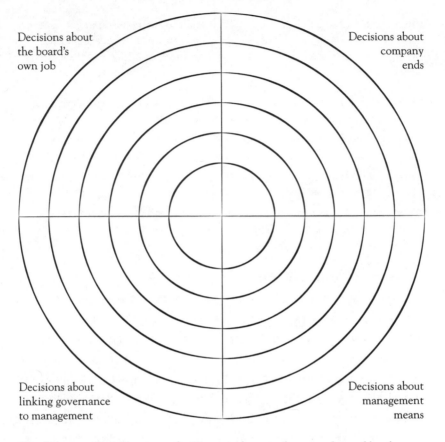

Decisions about the board's own job

Decisions about company ends

Decisions about linking governance to management

Decisions about management means

The four categories of corporate decisions are shown as four sets of nested bowls, brought together to form four quadrants of a circle. Again, larger and smaller issues within the categories are shown as larger and smaller bowls.

own board's requirements, and they will likely identify additional policies that their board might wish to create. We look in more detail at possible policies in later chapters but offer a brief introduction here.

It follows from what we have already discussed that the first policy in each category is a statement of the largest or broadest decision in that category. For example, the broadest level in Management Limitations might be stated this way: "Management shall not cause or allow any action or practice which is imprudent, unlawful, or unethical." Such a proscription is not specific as to

Figure 2.4. Visual Profile of Board Policy.

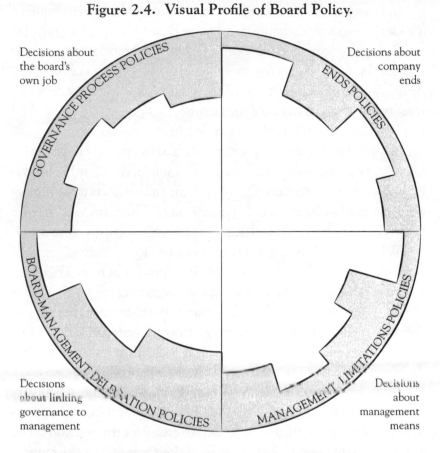

Decisions about
the board's
own job

GOVERNANCE PROCESS POLICIES

Decisions about
company
ends

ENDS POLICIES

BOARD-MANAGEMENT DELEGATION POLICIES

MANAGEMENT LIMITATIONS POLICIES

Decisions
about linking
governance to
management

Decisions
about
management
means

Completed board policies will occupy the outer part of each category (the largest
bowl) and will offer more detail, going into smaller bowl levels, on different topics
within each category. The contents of each level and amount of detail offered depend
on the board's values. The policy category containing all the operational means issues
is addressed by the board in a constraining or negative fashion, hence that category is
titled Management Limitations. The empty space in the middle represents all the
smaller decisions that the board is content to leave to its delegatees.

topic (such as financial management or human resources) but
applies globally to everything within management. A restriction of
this sort on corporate means is meaningful but extraordinarily
broad. The board would consider its corporate means policymaking complete at this point only if it were willing to accept the
accompanying full range of possibilities implied by the any reasonable interpretation rule described earlier.

If, however, this broadest level statement leaves to management a wider range of interpretation than the board is willing to grant (as in our experience all boards decide), then the board must go on to address the next lower (narrower) level and then, if necessary, the next lower level and so on until the board is willing to accept any reasonable interpretation of the narrower language. At the second level of definition in the Management Limitations quadrant, a number of topical issues naturally surface, such as treatment of personnel, financial risk, and asset protection. For example, the board's prohibition about asset protection might be, "Don't allow assets to be unnecessarily risked or inadequately maintained." Then, once again, the board decides whether it will stop at this level or go into more detail.

Wherever the board stops its policymaking, management is authorized to use the any reasonable interpretation rule. Therefore the board should resolve issues in each decision category in a disciplined sequence from the broadest toward the narrowest, but only to the point where it can accept any reasonable interpretation of its words. Board decisions made in this way logically contain all further decisions, whether or not the board ever knows of all those decisions.

In the same way that ends are expressed as the value a company intends to add for its owners, the most powerful way to describe jobs is in terms of the value they are intended to create for the company. The alternative is to describe jobs in terms of their activities. For example, a clerk's job could be described with a list of all the steps needed to file and safeguard records. But a description of the same clerk's job in terms of the value it adds might simply be *complete retrievability of records*. You will find that each of the jobs in our policy samples, be it the job of board, chair, board committee, or CEO, is expressed in this way.

Looking Back, Moving Forward

This chapter introduced the Policy Governance model, designed to be a theoretically coherent and practically applicable approach to board job design. The implications of the model for the role of the board, its officers, and its committees are the subject of the next chapter.

Chapter Three

Forging *Group* Leadership

The power of the board lies in its *collective wisdom*, which is released only when the board functions as a *collective body*.

—*Ram Charan*[1]

In This Chapter

- Converting directors into a board
- Assigning roles to the chair and committees
- Separating governance and management
- Creating Governance Process policies

The intent of the Policy Governance model is to bring greater precision to the challenge of translating owners' wishes into company performance. This precision is reflected not only in the policymaking process but in the roles of the various actors as well. In the last chapter we introduced specific policy categories. Using these four groupings the board can frame its decisions so that practice and documents are consistent with coherent governance design. In this chapter we are concerned with the policy category Governance Process. We set out key features of the board's special form of leadership, the roles of individuals and the group, and how these matters can be codified in a few brief policies.

The Board's Group Role

The first thing that sets the board's role apart from every other role in the company is that the board sits between owners and management. The second distinguishing feature is that the board's authority is *group* authority. Individual directors have no authority other than their influence in the group. There is no authority on or under the board that does not originate in the group's authority.

Directors are usually not accustomed to operating in this manner. Directors have typically achieved their professional and community status due to their individual accomplishments. They have a personal history of being decision makers *in their own right,* making decisions on their own immediate authority. In governance, however, in the *deliberation* leading to the exercise of governance authority, individuals matter absolutely. But in the *exercise* of authority (that is, in the actual taking of a decision) it is the group that matters; the individuals do not matter at all.

The values and perspectives of individual directors are the ingredients for group decisions. Even when informed or persuaded by others—such as management, lawyers, consultants, or bankers—it is the collected directors' wisdom that settles the vote. Directors as individuals have a responsibility to contribute actively, thoughtfully, and responsibly to the debate, but not to be individual supermanagers. It is in the whole that the value of the board lies.

The board role, then, requires that directors assume personal responsibility to behave so that the group *as a group* exercises authority and the group *as a group* bears accountability for the behavior of the entire company. Although other people can help directors with this challenge, no one can relieve them of it. Delegation becomes abdication unless the board fully owns and masters the phenomenon of group authority so as to remain completely accountable for any part of that authority it subsequently delegates to others.

Speaking as One Voice from Many

In speaking on behalf of the company's ownership, individual directors must speak with a single voice—to speak as one voice from many. The *many* are not just a multiple of directors but the often unwieldy number of owners. The board is obligated to insulate management from the many voices—whether of individual directors or owners—and to demand that management's loyalty be to the board's soberly considered summary of those voices.

Hence, only the board *speaking with one voice* instructs management. Management need not heed any director, but must accept the board's group decisions as if law. What any given director has to say on any given topic is of interest to other directors but need not be to management. Management is not confronted with, or later evaluated on, a laundry list of directors' individual wishes but only with the will of the group. Management can truly be said to work for no *one*.

Differentiating Advice from Instruction

Quite apart from their governance role, directors typically have a wealth of experience, wisdom, and expertise that management would be wasteful to ignore. The principle of group authority does not prevent individual directors from offering advice to management. Advice, as long as it is truly advice, has no instructive effect and so does not violate the one voice rule. Advice from directors should follow the *consenting adults* rule: as long as both parties agree to it, there is no harm done. Managers can distinguish advice from instruction with certainty, however, only when the directors, speaking as a group, explicitly make it clear that management has the right to ignore directors speaking as individuals. To leave this unclear is to impose political difficulties on management and to excuse the board from the discipline of good governance.

Directors often enjoy giving advice, and we do not seek to minimize their advisory contribution. What we must point out, however, is that advice to management is not the proper reason for the existence of a board of directors. The reason the board exists is to govern, a role with far greater responsibility than giving advice—and harder, too, we might add. Advising, asking good questions, criticizing management initiatives, and other director involvements require far less rigor than governing—at least governing of the quality that we describe.

Advising management, then, is a discretionary endeavor for directors, not the substance of their job. Excellent governance requires that boards put an end to the commonplace practice of putting more emphasis on optional individual director undertakings than on the mandatory group governance challenge.

The Value of Diversity and Dialogue

Getting to the point at which the single will of the group can be expressed calls for rich dialogue within the board among the directors with their multiple wills. On many issues it also requires extensive input from persons not on the board. Although the board's helpers and advisers are important to the dialogue, they should neither steer it nor be responsible for it. It falls to directors alone to undertake the struggle to transform individual wisdom, commitment, and discipline into group wisdom, commitment, and discipline. Boards must stimulate, embrace, and then resolve diversity, balancing the inclusion of widely different values and perspectives with the need to be decisive.

For some boards, assertively seeking and wrestling with diversity seems at odds with speaking with one voice. Whereas political and nonprofit boards frequently fall into diversity-driven fibrillation, it is more common for corporate boards to settle the dilemma by calling for unanimous votes. Governance at its best avoids both these outcomes. It considers multiple viewpoints to be priceless. It deems the ability to speak authoritatively and powerfully despite lack of total agreement to be one of a board's greatest strengths. It recognizes that unanimous votes are less about board solidarity and the demonstration of resoluteness than they are about political cover.

Corporate boards often feel that they need to show owners and managers a greater degree of unanimity than they actually possess. And there is no doubt that less than unanimous votes on highly sensitive and public issues can affect how these decisions are seen in the market. However, we urge boards to have real votes and, over time, to get the message across that they are always unanimous in their *support* of a final vote's absolute authority, whatever the diversity of viewpoints that arose in the discussion.

Practices That Weaken Board Authority

The board acts like a funnel through which the massive legitimacy of ownership is poured into a small group—with no leakage of power around the edges—before it is carefully passed on to others. Any arrangement or practice that detracts from the board's ability to faithfully play its role between the real owners and everyone else is an impediment to corporate governance. The problems of agency associated with having persons operate on behalf of others are difficult enough to deal with, given our human propensity for self-interest. The problems that arise from having structures or traditional practices that are inconsistent with uncomplicated board authority add considerably to the difficulty.

For example, board membership decided or significantly influenced by management compromises the board's independence. Board agendas established by management and board meetings stage-managed by management cause *governors to be managed by management* rather than *managers to be governed by governance*. Chair or executive committee power over the board means the board has failed to assume its authoritative *first cause* role. Combining chair and chief executive roles in the same person jeopardizes the crisp distinction between governance and management. These practices are commonplace, and there are many more.

Clarifying Other Governance Roles

The role of the board as a group must be the starting place for all role definitions throughout the company. Here, however, we are going to talk only of governance roles and in particular the roles of committees and the chair.

The Role of Board Committees

Board committees are subsets of the board as a whole. Therefore, by definition, they pose a potential threat to the board's wholeness and its ability to speak with one voice. When a board committee makes a decision that should belong to the whole board, the rest of the board has been disenfranchised. When part of the board has been disenfranchised, the board as a body has been disenfranchised. When the board as a body has been disenfranchised, the owners represented by the board have been disenfranchised. Consequently, as useful as committees can be, it is important to use them in such a way that board wholeness is not jeopardized or short-circuited.

Committees can play a useful part in governance as long as they never substitute for the full board's decision-making authority and never get between the board and management. The two appropriate uses of board committees are, first, to research options for full board decisions and, second, to carry out a delegated governance job, such as monitoring performance or arranging for monitoring performance. It is important, of course, that a committee is never given authority that overlaps authority given to management. It is also important that a committee is never given the right to judge management performance against its own, rather than the board's, criteria. Using committees can save the full board's time; however, boards should take care that such use does not fragment governance into committee fiefdoms or delude directors who are not on a given committee into thinking that they are relieved of the overall accountability.

Exhibit 3.1 offers a set of principles for board committees. Following these principles will keep board committees in line with the overall governance principles we have discussed (see Exhibit 1.1). In the following sections we discuss a few of the more frequently used board committees in the light of these principles for committees.

Executive Committees. Executive committees are frequently established to make decisions in the board's absence. However, any system that creates a *real* board within the full board does not bode

Exhibit 3.1. Principles for Board Committees and Officers.

- Function as part of and under the control of the board, not management
- Can have no authority that does not come from the board
- Can have no authority or accountability that is also delegated to management
- Cannot relieve the full board of its ultimate accountability for everything
- Cannot have the authority to instruct management
- Are always meant to help the board with some part of the governance job
- Are never meant to help or advise management
- Are charged to produce products (values added), not to engage in activities
- Have authority to use money or support personnel only if that is granted by the board

well for total board accountability. Even if the full board is asked later to sanction the committee decisions, by the time approval is requested it is likely to be a matter of form rather than substance. In any case, sanctioning others' work is not the same as exercising the board's highest and initial authority. In our experience, executive committees are typically put in place either because the full board is too large or because the time demanded by board service is too great for some directors. The solution to the former circumstance is to reduce the board's size. The solution to the latter may in part be more appropriate director recruitment. However, the more fundamental solution to unrealistic demands on directors is the better board job design offered by the Policy Governance framework.

Audit Committees. Audit committees are often created to correct for a board that is less independent of management than the integrity of its accountability to owners would demand. As with any other committee created for this purpose, the better solution is to make the full board properly independent to begin with.

Of course even a fully independent board may still choose to have an audit committee. When it does, what is the audit committee's job? Or, more accurately, what value is the audit committee to add that constitutes its reason for existence? First, in keeping with the principles for committees (Exhibit 3.1), the committee does not relieve the board of any responsibility whatsoever; it merely helps the board with that responsibility. Second, it has no authority to instruct management (except to gain unobstructed access to necessary records and personnel). What jobs are then left for an audit committee? One legitimate value-added the committee can produce for the board is a slate of competent external auditors from which shareholders can choose (a research role). Another is board knowledge of the degree to which the board's financial policies are being met by management (a monitoring role). Another is board assurance that the external auditor's scope includes any board policies for which the board wishes the auditor to assess compliance (an organizing of the monitoring role). Still another is board confidence that the external auditor has no conflicts due to management consulting or other factors (a monitoring role).

Compensation Committees. The compensation committee is another committee for which independence is important and to which the principles for committees apply. Possible values-added produced by compensation committees include the determination of the actual amounts and composition of CEO compensation (in relation to a reasonable interpretation of the preexisting, higher level policy on this matter that the board has determined in its decision-making role). Another legitimate value this committee could add is the determination of whether other management compensation complies with board policy relevant to compensation and benefits (a monitoring role). Still another is board understanding of the options for and implications of various approaches to management and director compensation (a research role).

Nominations Committees. A nominations committee that researches possible criteria for new directors and then searches for new directors who meet the criteria decided on by the board is adding legitimate value to the full board's role.

Advisory Committees. The need to differentiate between instruction and advice (as discussed earlier in this chapter) clearly applies to advisory committees. Here we distinguish advisory committees a board might establish to advise itself from advisory committees established to advise management. As to the former, the board may at any time create any advisory mechanism it wishes to help with its job. As to the latter, we strongly discourage forming board committees to advise management.

One reason for our objection is that managers are perfectly capable of finding their own advice. A second reason is that advice from directors officially assembled by the board can be difficult to distinguish from instruction. If managers are in charge of their own advisory mechanisms, then any directors who might show up on committees formed by management are less likely to get their advising and instructing roles confused. Any committees established by management have nothing to do with governance and need not be controlled by or officially related to the board in any way. We have never found a downside to a simple rule that boards should never create committees to advise or help management with anything.

The Role of the Chair

We believe that the chair's role is one of the most important keys to unlocking board potential, and we are therefore going to give it considerable attention. To begin with, we return to our point that no one in a company or on a board has any authority, or indeed any role at all, unless the board grants it. Governing authority is vested in a group of equals in which no one member has authority over another and certainly no one member has any authority over the group as a whole. But, given this fact, by what process then will the directors all have their say and their opportunity to convince? By what discipline beyond the persuasiveness of members' arguments will individuals be prevented from dominating the group? Who will safeguard the integrity of the process while members are engaged in forceful and thoughtful interchange?

The most obvious, and we believe most logical, mechanism for protecting and advancing the board in its work as a responsible group is the office of the chair. (We are reluctant to use the word *chairman* due to its gender specificity and the word *chairperson* due to its awkwardness. Please indulge our use of the almost equally awkward *chair*.) We are talking here about the role of the chair in relation to the board's process, *not* to the supervision of management. (We deal later with removing any management supervision connotations the role has acquired.)

Dealing with Groupness.   The chair role is created by an authoritative group that is unwilling to default on its group responsibility and that recognizes default will be likely if it operates without a leader. Necessary though the chair role is, however, if it is given too much authority, it can undermine the group's responsibility. Even when the board does not formally overempower the chair, there is the danger that it may do so unintentionally. In other words, the most common solution to the undisciplined tendencies of *groupness* is itself the greatest threat to achieving a responsible group. The purpose of the chair position is not to relieve the group of its difficult groupness but to help it deal competently with its group nature. The chair who "saves" the board from its responsibility is undermining the entire reason for the board's existence. A competent chair who keeps the board to its word is priceless.

Providing Servant-Leadership.   The chair works for the board, not the reverse. He or she becomes servant to the board in order to fulfil its group need for leadership. The chair's role is, on behalf of the board, to see to it that the board gets its job done. Philosophically, the guiding concept should be that of *servant-leadership*, as conceived by Robert Greenleaf.[2] The board chair is a leader, to be sure, but his or her leadership is legitimized only by its underlying servanthood.[3] The chair sees to it that the board runs itself, but he or she has authority only when acting within the domain delegated by the group. Directors, in effect, demand that the chair act in such a way that they as individuals can transform themselves into a responsible body.

Wielding the Gavel. Perhaps it is possible for a group without a leader to talk as a group, decide as a group, and discipline its interactions entirely as a group, but for most groups of assertive, energetic persons these accomplishments are unrealistic. Group paralysis, disarray, or dominance by a single powerful personality are almost inevitable dangers. The board needs assistance to achieve the discipline and integrity to which it is committed but for which as a leaderless group it would scarcely have the capability. The board needs the chair to wield the gavel and enforce the board's commitment to discipline while at no time becoming the group's superior.

The Role of Other Officers

The principles for other board officers, such as corporate secretaries or treasurers, are the same as those for committees (Exhibit 3.1). (Managers, be they the CEO or COO or CFO, are not governance officers and therefore not discussed here.)

Separating Governance and Management

The purpose and nature of board authority require that governance and management be treated differently. They are different roles, producing different values-added, requiring different skills, and addressing different levels of work. Failing to delineate clearly between these roles severely hinders effective governance.

The confounding of governance and management roles is most clearly illustrated in the common practice of assigning the roles of chair and CEO to the same person. These roles are both accountable to the board, but they cover different domains of authority and require different skills. The success of the chair can be judged by the effectiveness of governance; the success of the CEO can be judged by the effectiveness of management. The Policy Governance model does not require that the chair and the CEO be different persons, but *the model does require that the roles be kept separate even when these two positions are held by the same person*.

We believe most boards have a compelling need to strengthen the uniqueness of the chair's role as *chief governance officer*. Going further, we believe that adopting the position's role definition as the position's title (as has occurred with the titles of CEO, CFO, COO, and CIO) would have much more than a cosmetic effect and would powerfully reinforce a distinctive governance mentality. Therefore we recommend replacing the title *chair* with the title CGO. (Rather than use this unfamiliar title in our main discussion, however, we devote Appendix B to the case for a title change. Our appendixes also include further discussion of other topics related to the separation of governance and management. The implications of the Policy Governance model for separating the positions of chair and CEO, and the difficulties with the strategy of having a lead director, are addressed in Appendix C. The practice of including inside, or executive, directors on boards is questioned in Appendix D.)

Creating Governance Process Policies

In Chapter Two we described the policy architecture of Policy Governance and set out the four categories of policy that encompass all aspects of a company: Ends, Management Limitations, Board-Management Delegation, and Governance Process. In this section, we apply that architecture to the policies by which the board governs itself, that is, the Governance Process category (the upper-left quadrant of the policy circle in Figure 2.4).

In this and subsequent discussions of the various policy categories (and in Appendix E), we offer many sample policies. The principles from which the sample policies are derived (Exhibit 1.1) and the policy architecture itself (the categories, the decisions-within-decisions ordering, and the any reasonable interpretation rule) are integral to the model and cannot be changed without destroying the model's effectiveness. However, in content and in depth of detail, boards must make their policy statements their own. As they consider the sample statements offered in this book, directors may find either that they agree sufficiently with many of them to adopt them as is or that they need to make many changes. Use of the model and these samples is much like the use of a personal organizer or diary. If you want your daily life to work well, it is important that you use each section of your organizer for the purpose identified and put your entries under the right days. What each entry says, however, is an individual matter.

Governance Process policies constitute the board's decisions on the purpose and nature of governance, the role of the board, and the ways the board has resolved to fulfill that role. Governance Process policies are means policies (they cannot be ends policies, for a corporation does not exist to be well governed but to produce value for owners), but they need not be stated in the negative as are Management Limitations policies. It makes no sense for the board to control itself by the limit-setting method that works for governing management's means. The board must, after all, decide how to do its own job.

Consequently, although the nature of the board's work on Ends is to define and demand and its work on Management Limitations is to define and prohibit, its work on Governance Process policies (and also Board-Management Delegation policies, as we shall see in the next chapter) is to define and commit. Here we illustrate the policy design described in Chapter Two with two sample Governance Process policies.

Governance Commitment

The first sample Governance Process policy is titled "Governance Commitment" (Exhibit 3.2). Like all board policies, it begins at the broadest level (the largest nesting bowl in the Governance Process category) with an overarching, or global, statement about the board's purpose and on whose behalf the board does its job. The policy then goes down one level of specificity to address issues (points 1 to 11 in Exhibit 3.2) in the global statement. That is, the board has created eleven statements subordinate to the global one. Each of these substatements, though dealing with a separate subtopic, sits in the first bowl inside the global statement. Or to put it another way, each substatement sits at the same level in relation to the biggest bowl.

Exhibit 3.2. Governance Process Policy "Governance Commitment."

The purpose of the board, on behalf of the shareholders, is to see to it that the company (a) achieves appropriate results for shareholders, and (b) avoids unacceptable actions and situations.

1. **Accountability Philosophy.** The board's fundamental accountability is to the shareholders.

2. **Social Responsibility.** Although the board accepts as its primary obligation to operate in the best interests of shareholders, that fidelity is tempered by an obligation to the social order and good citizenship.

3. **Governing Style.** The board will govern lawfully with an emphasis on (a) outward vision rather than an internal preoccupation, (b) encouragement of diversity in viewpoints, (c) strategic leadership more than administrative detail, (d) clear distinction of board and chief executive roles, (e) collective rather than individual decisions, (f) the future rather than the past or present, and (g) proactivity rather than reactivity.

4. **Board Job Description.** The specific job outputs (values-added) of the board, as informed agent of the shareholders, are those that ensure an unbroken chain of accountability from shareholders to company performance.

5. **Board-Shareholder Linkage.** As the representative of the shareholders' interests, the board will maintain a credible and continuing link between owners and operators.

6. **Agenda Planning.** To accomplish its job products with a governance style consistent with board policies, the board will follow an annual agenda that (a) completes a reexploration of Ends policies annually, (b) reexamines Management Limitations policies and the sufficiency of their protection from risk, and (c) continually improves board performance through board education and enriched input and deliberation.

7. **Chair's Role.** The chair ensures the integrity of the board's process and, secondarily, represents the board as needed to outside parties, including but not limited to shareholders.

8. **Directors' Conduct.** The board commits itself and its members to ethical, businesslike, and lawful conduct, including members' proper use of authority and appropriate decorum when acting as directors.

9. **Committee Principles.** Board committees, when used, will be assigned so as to reinforce the wholeness of the board's job and so as never to interfere with delegation from board to CEO.

10. **Committee Structure.** Board committees are those set forth by board action, along with their job products, time lines, and board-authorized use of funds and management time. Unless otherwise stated, a committee ceases to exist as soon as its task is complete.

11. **Cost of Governance.** The board will consciously invest in its ability to govern competently and wisely.

Figure 3.1 illustrates the approximate profile of board policy once the policy "Governance Commitment" has been established. The outer level corresponds to the global statement; the second level corresponds to the numbered points. (Note that the figures that illustrate the levels of policy in this chapter and the next two chapters do not necessarily show exactly the same number of policy points as the particular policy samples that we have chosen to discuss.) Completing all the policies necessary to the Governance Process category might yield the fuller policy profile shown in Figure 3.2.

Chair's Role

Our second example of a Governance Process policy, "Chair's Role," is given in Exhibit 3.3. This policy sets out the authority and responsibility of the governance leader, whether called the chair or the chief governing officer.

Notice that the policy presented in Exhibit 3.3 is itself an extension of a subpart of the policy in Exhibit 3.2. Figure 3.2 illustrates that as the board goes into more detail in this and other policies in the Governance Process category, the subparts multiply. This phenomenon acts

Figure 3.1. Governance Process Policies: Levels One and Two.

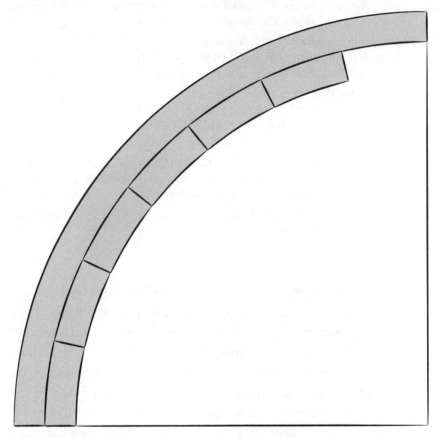

The board has created the global level and one further level of detail in its Governance Process policies.

as a brake on any tendency to race into greater detail. The stopping point that should be observed, of course, is the point at which the board is willing to allow its delegatee (in this case, the chair) to make any reasonable interpretation of the board's words.

Interpretation of Governance Process Policies

The authority to reasonably interpret board policy belongs to the chair not only for all Governance Process policies but also for all Board-Management Delegation policies, and this authority is itself explicitly set down in policy. When the board has made Gover-

Figure 3.2. Governance Process Policies Completed.

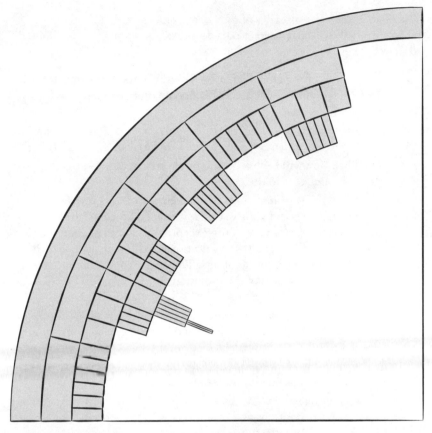

The board has established its Governance Process policies deeply enough that any decisions or choices made by a delegatee will be acceptable to the board if they are a reasonable interpretation of the broader statements. Thus the board can now safely delegate all further decisions in this category.

nance Process decisions in whatever detail it wishes (descending to whatever size bowl in the nested set it sees fit), the board authorizes its chair to make all further decisions on that topic, as long as the chair's decisions are a reasonable interpretation of the board's words.

Appendix E presents samples of policies in all four policy categories, often moving down at least one level further than that shown in Figure 3.1, and in some cases two levels. Governance Process policy samples in Appendix E cover, among other topics, the board's accountability and governing style, its job products, the

Exhibit 3.3. Governance Process Policy "Chair's Role."

The chair ensures the integrity of the board's process and, secondarily, represents the board as needed to outside parties, including but not limited to shareholders.

1. The job result of the chair is that the board behaves consistently with its own rules and those legitimately imposed on it from outside the organization.
   A. Meeting discussion content will be only those issues that according to board policy clearly belong to the board to decide, not to the CEO.
   B. Deliberation will be fair, open, and thorough, but also timely, orderly, and kept to the point.
2. The authority of the chair consists in making decisions that fall within topics covered by board policies on Governance Process and Board-Management Delegation, with the exception of (a) employment or termination of a CEO and (b) any portions of this authority that the board specifically delegates to others. The chair is authorized to use any reasonable interpretation of the provisions in Governance Process and Board-Management Delegation policies.
   A. The chair is empowered to chair board meetings with all the commonly accepted power of that position (for example, ruling, recognizing).
   B. The chair has no authority to make decisions about or within the Ends and Management Limitations policy areas.
   C. The chair may represent the board to outside parties in announcing board-stated positions and in stating decisions and interpretations in the area delegated to her or him.
   D. The chair may delegate any part of his or her authority to another director but remains accountable for its use.

role of the chair as chief governance officer, the conduct of individual directors, and committee principles.

Looking Back, Moving Forward

We have addressed how the board can be responsible for its own performance as a group, but that means nothing unless the board impacts the performance of the company. The next chapter examines how the board can drive company performance through one employee, its CEO.

Chapter Four

Connecting to Management

What is needed is a vibrant alternative way to
ensure that power is exercised, over every type and
form of corporate entity . . . in a way that ensures
both effective performance and appropriate social
accountability and responsibility.

—Robert I. Tricker[1]

In This Chapter

- Why management performance is the CEO's performance
- Why the CEO's only boss is the board's group voice
- Understanding the board-CEO relationship and delegation principles
- Creating Board-Management Delegation policies

Boards can directly control their own performance, but they cannot produce total company performance on their own. This chapter explains how boards can give extensive authority to management and yet remain fully accountable for the ways that authority is used.

Delegating Authority to Management

To translate owners' wishes into company performance, boards must give most of their authority away. Corporate performance requires massive delegation and powerful management. Unless the board wishes to become the management team as well as the governance group, it must drive company performance in such a way that management is not only challenged but empowered. The first questions confronted, however, as the board connects to management are whom to instruct, whom to empower, and whom to hold accountable.

The CEO as the Board's Single Management Employee

It is possible for a board to govern a company without having management authority and accountability come to a focus in a single individual such as a CEO. Very few boards choose to do this, however, for the wisdom of having a chief executive is hard to fault. At least, very few boards choose to do this *intentionally*.

There are many cases in which a chair assumes some of the named CEO's authority. In such cases the board allows the CEO role to be diluted and its value in the chain of accountability to be destroyed. When a board chooses to use the CEO function, it must do so 100 percent. There is no such thing as a partial CEO. When the board delegates to more than one manager, it puts itself in the position of supermanager and is therefore delegating only some tasks rather than total authority and accountability for management performance.

Policy Governance calls for the board to delegate authority for all management performance to the chief executive officer *function*. In other words, whatever the position title (president, general manager, managing director, CEO, or the like) and whatever additional role might be assigned to the same person (for example, the chair role), powerful delegation to management requires the *function* that we are, for the remainder of this book, calling CEO.

The CEO is the link in the chain of command that connects the board to the rest of management. Therefore, in giving instructions and judging performance, the board speaks with *one* group voice only to this *one* person. The board delegates to this one person the authority to manage everyone else in the operating structure. So when the CEO speaks officially to his or her colleagues, he or she speaks—as far as they are concerned—with the authority of the board.

Given this clear line of authority, the board can and should hold the CEO alone accountable for what is done with the delegated executive authority. All operational achievements, conduct, decisions, and situations are on that person's head. Management performance *is* CEO performance. The board has only one employee—the CEO. The CEO has only one boss—the board's one group voice.

A Powerful CEO Is in the Board's Interest

The board is obligated to the owners for successful company performance—therefore the board cannot be successful unless its CEO is successful. The CEO cannot be successful unless he or she has the power to make things happen. In other words, it is to the board's advantage to have a strong CEO, not a weakened one.

The Policy Governance model calls for boards to give their CEOs as much authority as possible, short of "giving away the shop." Once the board has established its role as commanding and evaluating the CEO's performance, its philosophy of delegation should place the burden of justification on holding back authority, not on granting it.

Responsibly maximizing management authority does not diminish the importance of governance but locates power for company performance where it can do the most good. Board delegation should model the kind of delegation the board would expect to find in a well-run company—delegation as thorough as possible without losing control.

Companies today must create value faster than ever before. Survival may depend on the CEO's ability to adjust quickly to sudden marketplace shifts. Global competition serves to create a challenging, rapidly changing business environment, as do customer demands for quick turnarounds, immediate access, and custom solutions. Quicker decisions are both enabled by new technology and demanded by the environment. This is no time and the board-CEO relationship is no place for cumbersome structures or practices. The board, in its own interest, must secure maximum CEO empowerment—and at the same time not jeopardize its own accountability to owners.

The CEO's Job Description

Within the Policy Governance framework, the CEO's job description, the value that the CEO adds, becomes very simple. *The CEO's job is to see to it that the company achieves the ends the board has established and avoids the unacceptable means the board has identified.* The CEO's job, then, is to ensure that the company complies with the two categories of board policy that address management (as opposed to board) performance. This is of course a simple summary of a very difficult job. But if the board holds the CEO accountable for compliance with this job description, it has all it needs to drive company performance and, in its turn, be accountable to owners for that performance.

Let us clarify the way we distinguish accountability from responsibility. *Responsibility* refers to an individual's or a group's direct, hands-on obligation to produce something of value. *Accountability* refers to an individual's or a group's obligation to *either* produce *or* see to the production of something of value. Hence one could say the board is accountable for customer service, but frontline staff are responsible for it. Moreover, the board is responsible for writing its policies whereas the CEO is responsible for interpreting them. The distinction between one's direct responsibility and one's responsibility for the achievements of subordinates is an important one in designing the board's job or the job of any manager. Whether one uses *responsibility* and *accountability* to label these two concepts or one uses *hands-on responsibility* and *hands-off responsibility*, the distinction must be made.

It follows therefore that the board does not care what the CEO takes responsibility for—it is his or her choice what responsibilities to delegate to whom and which to retain. After all, the organizational chart is itself a managerial means decision with which the board would be well advised not to interfere. What the board does care about is the CEO's *accountability*—that is, the cumulative total of all the responsibilities within the company (other than the responsibility of the board for its own conduct). And that cumulative total adds up to two things: (1) the company achieves whatever form of shareholder value or other benefit for owners that the board has decided and (2) the company avoids unacceptable risks, methods, conduct, and situations.

Practices That Weaken Delegation to Management

When other managers such as the chief financial officer or chief operating officer sit at the board table (as directors or in other positions), the *one employee* principle may be in danger. The board must be careful not to give, or seem to give, these officers direct instructions. When this happens, the board is implying that these other managers are its direct employees too, thereby diluting the role of the CEO.

Another set of problems is created when the board fails to speak with one group voice. When the chair (or indeed any other director) holds the CEO directly accountable to himself or herself, the chair to some degree becomes the de facto CEO. In other words, the chair becomes the board's link to management performance and thus should be the person the board holds accountable for that performance. It is difficult, however, for a board to hold its chair to account for the CEO's responsibilities, and the board's relationship with the person who actually carries the CEO title becomes confused.

Delegation is also weakened when the CEO does not feel secure about taking the board at its word. In such cases the CEO must either risk possible board disapproval of managerial decisions or return to the board for repeated approvals. This can result in a reticent CEO who continually takes the precaution of drawing the board into managerial decisions and issues or a CEO who takes control of the board process through manipulation and agenda setting in order to protect his or her turf.

Finally, when the board tells the CEO how to do his or her job (thereby prescribing management's means), the CEO's latitude to plan and implement the company's operations is reduced, and delegation is therefore weakened. Further, if the board dictates the choice of some or all of the means to achieve the ends, it cannot logically hold the CEO fully accountable for the achievement of those ends.

The Policy Governance model addresses all these potential weaknesses in delegation to management and eliminates any lack of clarity about the fact that the board delegates to management, never the other way round.

The Board-CEO Relationship

The board's accountability to owners is constant; the board is a permanent authority. Board leadership therefore should be constantly and consistently applied. A proper board is not a crisis, standby authority. It does not exist to help management, to duplicate management, or to fill in weaknesses of management. Proper governance exists to exercise an ongoing authority, establishing values that drive the company through all its known and yet to be known challenges. Management's job is to apply those values to the company's operation in a world of shifting conditions, opportunities, and threats.

Although the board's authority is clearly superior to the CEO's authority, in practice there is considerable partnership. The CEO has a vested interest in ensuring that the board's decisions are wise ones, for the board and the CEO will have to live by them and be evaluated according to them, not just today but every day for the foreseeable future. The board has a vested interest in seeking the CEO's input, for its success is dependent upon his or her success. As in a sport, maximum productive interchange—playing and working together—is possible only when the roles and rules are not in doubt.

Good relationships are built on trust. The board increases trust between itself and its CEO by creating fair expectations and judging only according to those expectations. Establishing policies and then ignoring them (in other words, saying one thing and doing another) damages trust. Failing to state in advance what is expected and then criticizing in hindsight damages trust. We are not talking here about the "over to you, but please don't give us any nasty surprises" kind of trust. Nor do we mean the "you know your job best" kind of trust. We don't even mean the "we're all in this thing together" kind of trust. We are talking about trust built on explicit roles, explicit expectations, and explicit monitoring.

The proper relationship between the chair and the CEO also must be clear. The chair and CEO are both charged by the board with considerable authority and obligations for leadership. The two roles are not hierarchically related, for each works directly for the board. The CEO does not report to the chair but to the board; the chair has no authority over the CEO. If this is not true, the chair is in effect the CEO, regardless of titles. Even when the same person holds both roles, it is important for directors as well as the incumbent to recognize and play each role out separately. The chair's job—as charged by the board—is to see that the board gets its job done. The CEO's job—as charged by the board—is to see to it that management gets its job done.

Delegation Principles

For delegation to work well it has to be overt and clear, realistic, and fairly judged. These are not mere technicalities but principles of natural justice that the Policy Governance model upholds.

- *Delegation must be overt and clear.* The Policy Governance framework requires that the board never hold the CEO accountable for meeting performance expectations that have not been stated. Therefore the board's policies must commit all the board's performance expectations to writing. The

model's method enables boards to do so succinctly, so com-
pleteness does not imply weighty documents.

- *Delegation must be realistic.* The board cannot rationally hold
  the CEO accountable for policies that are not realistic. If
  policies are not realistic, they become useless, valued more
  for their rhetorical flourish than their stated purpose. The
  board must therefore ensure that it is sufficiently informed
  to know what is and is not realistic, and it needs to review
  its expectations regularly to ensure that they remain doable.

- *Delegation must be fairly judged.* As a matter of fair play, the
  board cannot judge the CEO without having first made its
  criteria known. Neither can the board allow the CEO to be
  criticized by a director for not meeting that individual director's expectations. Directors as a body are obligated to protect
  the CEO from directors as individuals.

Creating Board-Management Delegation Policies

We have chosen three policies to illustrate how the Policy Governance architecture frames the board's delegation to the CEO in the
Board-Management Delegation category. (A fuller set of samples
can be seen in Appendix E.)

Delegation to the CEO

The first sample policy (Exhibit 4.1), titled "Delegation to the
CEO," begins with the most global level of decision then progresses
into more detail one level at a time. Its preamble expresses the
board's broadest level decision about the governance-management
connection, declaring that the board will govern the company
through the CEO, who will be its "sole official connection" with
the company. The word *official* leaves open the possibility of informal relationships with others. In subparts 1 through 6, the board
addresses the level immediately below the broadest level, spelling
out, still at a rather broad level, the implications of having only one

Exhibit 4.1. Board-Management Delegation Policy "Delegation to the CEO."

The board's sole official connection to the operational company, its achievements, and its conduct will be through a chief executive officer (CEO).

1. **Unity of Control.** Only officially passed motions of the board, speaking authoritatively as a group, are binding on the CEO.

2. **Accountability of the CEO.** The CEO is the board's only official link to operational achievement and conduct, so that all authority and accountability of management is considered by the board to be the authority and accountability of the CEO.

3. **Nature of CEO Delegation.** The board will instruct the CEO through written policies that prescribe the shareholder benefit to be achieved and describe organizational situations and actions to be avoided, allowing the CEO any reasonable interpretation of these policies.

4. **Monitoring CEO Performance.** Systematic and rigorous monitoring of CEO job performance will be solely against the provisions of the board's Ends policies and Management Limitations policies.

5. **CEO Compensation.** CEO compensation will be decided by the board as a body and based on company performance and executive market conditions.

6. **CEO Termination.** CEO termination is an authority retained by the board and not delegated to any officer or committee.

employee and the way it will delegate to and monitor the performance of that employee.

Figure 4.1 shows approximately how the "Delegation to the CEO" policy would appear on the policy circle. Its preamble (global opening statement) establishes the largest thought of the Board-Management Delegation category. Its numbered parts go one level into detail.

Accountability of the CEO

The second sample policy (Exhibit 4.2), "Accountability of the CEO," deals with the board's intention to establish airtight CEO accountability and illustrates a further level of specificity, taking as its point of departure the second substatement in the "Delegation

Figure 4.1. Board-Management Delegation Policies: Levels One and Two.

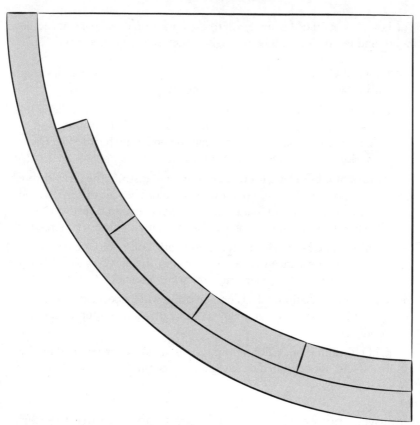

The board has created the global level and one further level of detail in its Board-Management Delegation policies.

to the CEO" policy. It refers to the CEO's job description as the accomplishment of the board's Ends policies and compliance with the board's policies on unacceptable means. We look at these policies in detail in the next chapter.

Monitoring Performance

Policy Governance demands that accountable delegation consist of, first, stating expectations; second, unambiguously assigning them to someone; and finally, monitoring or evaluating perfor-

Exhibit 4.2. Board-Management Delegation Policy "Accountability of the CEO."

The CEO is the board's only official link to operational achievement and conduct, so that all authority and accountability of management is considered by the board to be the authority and accountability of the CEO.

1. The board will never give instructions to persons who report directly or indirectly to the CEO.

2. The board will not evaluate, either formally or informally, the job performance of any management position other than the CEO.

3. The board will view CEO performance as identical to total management performance, so that organizational accomplishment of board-stated Ends and avoidance of board-stated Management Limitations will be viewed as successful CEO performance. No performance measure established by the board or by organs of the board (such as a compensation committee) shall conflict with or modify this measure of performance.

4. All Management Limitations imposed on the CEO are limitations imposed on all management, so that violation by any part of the company is a violation by the CEO.

mance against those expectations. Policies created within the Policy Governance framework form the stated expectations, and their wording sets the stage for measurable monitoring after the CEO has produced an interpretation. The whole topic of monitoring and evaluation is considered in far more depth in Chapter Six. For now we present the board policy that describes this feature of Board-Management Delegation.

This policy (Exhibit 4.3), "Monitoring CEO Performance," is essential to building the proper reporting relationship between the board and CEO. The board requires that its words be acted upon and tracks that they are in fact acted upon. When the board does not take full responsibility for monitoring the CEO's fulfillment of its policies—which translates into how board-granted authority is being used—it has abdicated its accountability.

When the board has created all the policies it feels are necessary to describe the governance-management relationship, the profile of

Exhibit 4.3. Board-Management Delegation Policy "Monitoring CEO Performance."

Systematic and rigorous monitoring of CEO job performance will be solely against the provisions of the board's Ends policies and Management Limitations policies.

1. Monitoring is simply to determine the degree to which board policies are being met. Data that do not do this will not be considered monitoring data.

2. The board will acquire monitoring data by one or more of three methods: (a) by internal report, in which the CEO discloses compliance information to the board, (b) by external report, in which an external, disinterested third party selected by the board assesses compliance with board policies, and (c) by direct board inspection, in which one or more designated members of the board assess compliance with the appropriate policy criteria.

3. In every case the standard for compliance shall be *any reasonable CEO interpretation* of the board policy being monitored. The board is the final arbiter of reasonableness but will always judge with a "reasonable person" test rather than with interpretations favored by individual directors or by the board as a whole.

4. All policies that instruct the CEO will be monitored at a frequency and by a method chosen by the board. The board can monitor any policy at any time by any method but will ordinarily depend on a routine schedule.

POLICY	METHOD	FREQUENCY
Ends		
Shareholder Value	Internal (CEO)	Annually
Management Limitations		
Basic Executive Constraints	External (various)	Annually
Treatment of Stakeholders	Internal (CEO)	Annually
Treatment of Employees	Internal (CEO)	Annually
Financial Planning and Budgeting	Internal (CEO)	Quarterly
Financial Condition and Activities	Internal (CEO) External (Auditor)	Quarterly Annually

POLICY	METHOD	FREQUENCY
Asset Protection	External (Auditor)	Annually
Short-Term CEO Succession	Direct inspection (Chair)	Annually
Investments	External (Auditor)	Semiannually
Compensation and Benefits	Internal (CEO)	Annually
Trading in Company Securities	Internal (CEO)	Semiannually
Communication and Support	Direct inspection (Chair)	Annually
Diversification	Internal (CEO)	Semiannually

5. Periodic evaluation of the CEO and the evaluation-based component of any CEO compensation decision by the board will be based on performance as demonstrated by the monitoring system described in this policy.

the resulting set of policies might resemble the depiction in Figure 4.2. (Some of the policies just described and some of the additional Board-Management Delegation policies in Appendix E will be more understandable in light of our explanations in the next chapter.)

Interpretation of Board-Management Delegation Policies

Board-Management Delegation policies, like Governance Process policies, deal with board means—in this case the means by which the board delegates authority to the CEO and demands accountability for its use. Because these policies directly govern board action rather than CEO action, the power of reasonable interpretation belongs to the chair. That authority of the chair is itself explicitly set down in policy (Exhibit 3.3). So when the board has written Board-Management Delegation policies in whatever detail it wishes (descending to whatever size bowl in the nested set it sees fit), the board authorizes its chair to make all further decisions on that topic, as long as the chair's decisions are a reasonable interpretation of the board's words.

Figure 4.2. Board-Management Delegation Policies Completed.

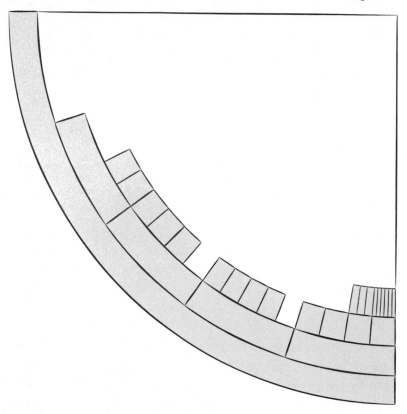

The board has established its Board-Management Delegation policies deeply enough that any decisions or choices made by a delegatee will be acceptable to the board if they are a reasonable interpretation of the broader statements. Thus the board can now safely delegate all further decisions in this category.

Looking Back, Moving Forward

This chapter has shown how the board can give the CEO the authority he or she needs to produce management performance and be accountable for that performance. The board has now established the roles and mechanics involved in the board-management linkage. But it has not provided the *content* of its expectations of management performance and therefore of the CEO's performance. The next chapter explains how the board can give the CEO explicit information about the kind of performance it expects.

Chapter Five

Setting Expectations for Management Performance

It is for the board, representing the interests of
those who appoint them, to set the standards
which they expect from the managers and to set
them high.

—*Sir Adrian Cadbury*[1]

In This Chapter

- How the board prescribes company ends
- How the board proscribes company means
- Creating Ends and Management Limitations policies

In Chapter Four we established the CEO function as the board's
sole instrument for driving management performance. Now we are
going to demonstrate how the Policy Governance framework
allows the board to create a powerful and precise instruction manual for that performance.

What the Company Is For

Company performance is a term that covers potentially every aspect
of a company. Company performance is about share price, employee
turnover, customer satisfaction, use of space, and numerous other

matters. All these matters are important, and the board faces the challenge of creating instructions for the management performance necessary to fulfill the board's accountability.

Within the Policy Governance framework the first step toward meeting this challenge is to identify what the company is *for*. The board cannot define what it wants its policies to say until it can define what it wants the company to achieve. The answer to the question, What is the company for? forms the central message to the CEO. It describes why he or she has a job. It constitutes the overall criterion for judging company and therefore CEO performance.

In addition, as we stated in Chapter Two, Policy Governance design requires the separation of the reason for a company's existence from everything else (ends from means) so that the board can separate nested sets of policies into compatible nested sets of decisions-within-decisions for delegation.

The Reason for Corporate Existence: To Produce Value for Owners

We assert that companies exist first and foremost for producing value for owners. In other words, an organization is *for* whatever its owners want it to be for, whereas it *does* what is necessary to fulfill what it is for. Different owners have different wants. Therefore each board needs not only to be clear about who its owners are but to have some degree of dialogue with them before it can specify the kind of value their company should produce. This process may be straightforward. Company owners are usually defined as shareholders, and they generally want to see value show up in their shares; but as discussed in Chapter Two, there can be exceptions to this point of view. Although most shareholders define the value they seek in purely financial terms, there are also shareholders who seek other benefits from their investment, such as the satisfaction of pioneering a particular breakthrough, supporting a particular kind of corporate behavior, or, where the owner is also the operator, working in a particular way.

Obligations to Other Stakeholders

A company also has responsibilities to people other than owners, but because those obligations are not part of the company's reason for being, our position is that they are not ends issues. All obligations other than to provide value to owners are means issues rather than ends issues. Therefore a board will choose whatever degree of care it wishes with regard to stakeholders other than owners, but that concern will be expressed in policies that limit the range of acceptable management behavior and board behavior. That is, it will be expressed in Management Limitations and Governance Process policies rather than in Ends policies.

A further look at the board's relationships with some particular groups of stakeholders supports the assertion that the board's obligations to nonowners are means obligations.

Legal Obligation. Public policy and law establish the minimum social responsibility of the corporation. The social order can choose to establish minimum wages, safety standards, discrimination safeguards, or parental leave. There is plenty of room for argument about the sensible limits of such impositions—argument based on political and economic philosophy as well as pragmatics—but the state is within its authority to make such choices. Subservience to the law is the board's fundamental social responsibility, but it has nothing to do with what the company is *for*. Lawfulness is a requirement of doing business, but the company does not exist so that the law can be fulfilled. The corporation's formal responsibility to the law is the clearest example of a board obligation that does not relate to ends.

Ethical Obligation. Ethical behavior too is a social responsibility, though with a greater breadth of interpretation and less obvious enforcement. There are many actions a company could take that would be acceptable under law but would fly in the face of many people's notions of common decency. The board might impose on the company the obligation to act ethically not because the board is required to do so but because it simply believes either that ethical behavior is right or that the business consequences of unethical behavior would be unacceptable.

Obligation to Consumers, Employees, and Suppliers. The board's obligation to consumers, employees, and suppliers is not to provide them with ownership value but to treat them with proper respect, legally and ethically. There are some companies that also have obligations to consumers, employees, and suppliers as owners. For example, the owners of cooperatives are also their customers, and some kinds of companies count their employees among their owners, owing to either share compensation schemes or special governance arrangements. Where there is such overlap, the board needs to clearly distinguish its obligation to people as owners from its obligation to the same people as consumers, employees, or suppliers, and the obligation to owners must always be paramount.

Wider Social Obligation. The term *corporate social responsibility* has come to include voluntary contributions of all sorts to the benefit of wider society, including support for the arts, social services, and local communities. The company does not exist to fulfill such an obligation, but the board may still decide to make such contributions as a means of enhancing the company's long-term interests or fulfilling the board's interpretation of ethical social behavior.

Commanding Ends

If ends are expressions of owner value rather than the values of other stakeholders, it is clear on whose behalf the board needs to create its Ends policies. Thus Ends policies must express the board's performance expectations with respect to appropriate benchmarks of corporate success *from the owners' perspective*.

The Three Components of Ends

Like all Policy Governance policy work, ends definition requires precision. However, it also requires an understanding of the power of expressing ends as the difference a corporation will make for owners (and not as the activities it will engage in to make that difference). To create statements that will most surely focus the entire company on producing the desired ends, the board must define three components in its ends concept: first, the *results* for which the corporation exists; second, the *recipients* of those results; and third, the *relative worth* of those results.

Defining the Results

In a company organized for profit, the results component of the ends relates ordinarily to the financial value that accrues to the company owners; that is, results are what is commonly referred to as shareholder value. However, there can be variations. In some small start-up companies, for example, desired results may include working independently with trusted partners in an exciting field—plus satisfactory financial return. In some family-owned companies, the value owners want is the satisfaction of having family members working together in the same business—plus satisfactory financial return.

The board's judgment here must take account of not only the type of results to be achieved but also the level of ambition they reflect and the time line for achieving them, all subjects on which different owners may have different views.

Defining the Recipients

If the desired results are expressions of owner value, then, by definition, the owners are the recipients. However, owners do not all have the same interests, and the board represents all owners. Boardroom debate must honor the diversity in the ownership, coming to conclusions that can be translated into expectations for company performance.

For smaller, closely held companies, deciding on recipients can be relatively straightforward, whereas that decision can get complicated for larger companies. The potential variety of perspectives on the question, Whom do we intend to benefit? is illustrated by

Robert A. G. Monks,[2] who argues that pensioners are the share-holders whose interests should be most served.

Defining the Relative Worth

To formulate the company's ends, having considered possible results and the range of owner-recipient desires, the board decides on the relative worth of the various desired results. In choosing one definition of result over another, the board is choosing the wishes of some owners over others and thus some results over others. For this reason, defining the relative worth component is the culmination of the board's decisions on the other two components.

For example, achieving the long-term, high results desired by one class of shareholder may seem of sufficient value to justify also accepting short-term, low results that another class of shareholder wishes to avoid. Much of the leadership contribution of a board comes from an ability to stand back and look at the bigger and longer term picture. The board's ends decisions have implications not only for focusing the company's entire effort but also for identifying the kinds of limitations that the board will subsequently impose on management. For example, a board that is building long-term owner value is going to be especially interested in ensuring that the company uses prudent and ethical means in its finances as well as in relationships with customers, employees, suppliers, and the wider community.

It is not for us to say what ends are right for any given board. The choices involved are often difficult, but responsible boards cannot choose *not* to make them. Here are a variety of financially oriented owner value definitions, stated at the broadest level to provide concrete examples of Ends policies that encompass all three ends components.

- Increased share price plus dividends constitutes no less than _____ return on shareholder investment.

- Ranking falls in the top third of companies in the creation of shareholder returns over full cycles as long as those returns are higher than the cost of capital.

- Compounded growth in annual earnings per share becomes no less than _____ by the year _____ and thereafter.

- Share price moves at a rate that exceeds the share price growth rate (or is less than the price decline rate) of a weighted composite index of the top four competitors.

- Return on equity constitutes at least _____ per year on a rolling four-quarter cycle.

These illustrate the kinds of culminating statements a board might create after having explicitly or implicitly considered the relative worth of different results and different recipients. We recommend that a board consider all the components explicitly, for only then can the board claim to be exercising its authority to lead the company in a thoughtful and deliberate manner.

Limiting Management's Means

Although corporate ends form the crux of the board's expectations of its CEO, they are not the only part. For in using the authority granted by the board to pursue ends, the CEO and his or her subordinates will make uncountable decisions about methods, practices, activities, and conduct of business. What is the best way to capitalize a venture? How should the organizational chart be arranged? Should the company produce nearer to raw materials or nearer to markets? Should it own or lease its fleet? Should it make or buy this component? How conciliatory should it be with union demands? Should it self-insure? Personnel, accounting, manufacturing, product design, marketing, and compensation plans are all means. The company exists for none of this vast and complex range of things, yet all of them are critical to company success.

The Effectiveness of Means Shows in the Ends

Most decisions made in a company are means decisions, and most employees are employed because of their expertise in dealing with specific means. Yet to the owners, means in themselves have no fundamental value. If acceptable shareholder value is not produced, owners will find little satisfaction in knowing that the compensation plan is the cleverest in the business or that the flow of goods-in-process on the plant floor is a design of pure genius. From the owners' perspective, the company gets no credit for means, only for ends. Reflecting this harsh reality in its role as the owners' voice, the board must give the CEO no points for means, only for ends. If ends are met, it must conclude that the means sufficed. The success of means in terms of producing desired ends, then, is judged not by looking at the means but at the ends.

But Some Means Are Always Unacceptable

In theory, therefore, a board that wanted to control only what it *must* (rather than all that it *can*) would simply define and demand ends performance, measure and reward that performance, and call the governance task done. That would be the case if *effectiveness* of means were the only concern. It is not that simple, of course, because *some effective means are not acceptable for reasons of ethics or probity.*

Frankly, corporations get into financial, legal, and social trouble due quite as often to their means as to their failure in creating adequate shareholder value. Imprudent investments or capital purchases, shady accounting practices, environmentally destructive waste disposal, and a myriad of other sins can lead to massive corporate embarrassment and distress. So the board has a need to exercise control over corporate means after all.

Drawing Boundaries Around Management's Means

The best way for a board to identify the means that it wants to control is to ask itself: What management situations, activities, or decisions would be unacceptable to us even if they worked? Even if ends are being achieved, what risks, ethical violations, and improprieties does the board want to put off limits? The board then expresses all its limitations on management's authority as verbal negatives—as "thou shalt nots." This enables the board, once it limits everything it believes necessary to limit, to give the CEO the positive message that everything else is in effect preauthorized. In other words, if the board has not said some situation, activity, conduct, or decision is unacceptable, it is automatically acceptable ("if we haven't said you can't, you can"). Instead of being granted authority in specific bits and pieces by the board, the CEO is granted all authority except what the board expressly prohibits. And of course, limiting the CEO limits the entire company, not just the CEO personally.

In our experience, knowing clearly what the board finds unacceptable (and thus expresses negatively) is experienced by CEOs as psychologically positive. The CEO then knows that as long as the boundaries defined in Management Limitations policies are observed, anything he or she does is acceptable. Moreover, the CEO does not have to live with the truly uncomfortable feeling of having an axe hanging over his or her head, an axe that can be wielded at a moment's notice for unpredictable reasons. The Policy Governance concept of bounded freedom arising out of carefully crafted, broadly based proscriptions optimizes board control and CEO latitude simultaneously.

Preserving Management Creativity and Agility

CEOs function best when impediments, including unnecessary director and board intrusion, are minimized. They work best with a free hand to make decisions, try new approaches, delegate extensively to their subordinates, and react quickly to unforeseen opportunities and threats. The more the board is involved in such decisions, the greater its risk of developing the features of a committee-as-CEO. Prescriptive control of the CEO's means is the most oppressive and management-damaging kind of control a board can exercise. As corporate boards are counseled by a developing literature to become more active, it will be a pity if directors feel they need to exercise direct involvement in management's decisions or get dragged into the approval syndrome.

Approval syndrome describes the common practice in which the CEO submits each plan to the board in order to have it approved. If the board retains approval authority over a topic, it presumably retains disapproval authority as well. However, in common approval practices the board has not stated the criteria by which it judges a plan approvable or disapprovable. In other words, the CEO's plan is being judged against criteria never stated or never stated completely. Moreover, even after approval, it is typically not clear what the criteria were, for the board does not vote on the criteria but on the document. The CEO knows the board is pleased, but must guess about what would have been displeasing.

As a general rule, boards retain approval authority when they have not done the work of delineating the criteria of approvability. When a board goes to the trouble of reading, studying, and approving, it is not a sign that it is doing its proper work. It is a sign the proper work has not been done. If governance work—as we define it here—has been done, the CEO will know all the requirements to begin with. Board inspection of the matter, if needed at all, is then focused completely on a few aspects—the ones the board wishes to control enough that it has created criteria (in the form of policy language) ahead of time. This approach avoids both rubber stamping (when the board does not take the approval process seriously) and micromanagement (when directors forage about in whatever parts of a document interest them).

The Policy Governance approach to controlling managerial means, then, can be said this way: although the board should state the expected ends prescriptively, *it should stay out of management's means except to prohibit those that would be unacceptable*. This method of control is similar to allowing a horse all the scampering about it wishes as long as it stays in the paddock—as opposed to leading it around by a rope and dictating where it stands or, to strain the analogy, requiring that the horse get the cowhand's approval for wherever it wishes to stand.

Acquiring Information for Creating Policies

Creating Ends and Management Limitations policies that cover every aspect of company performance is a tall order indeed, especially given the wide range of subjects to be covered and the board's distance from day-to-day company action. The board's policy decisions have to be appropriately informed, yet it may seem difficult for a board to ensure that it is informed *enough*. We go further into the topic of board information requirements in the next chapter, but we are introducing it briefly here because information is such an important issue in determining both ends and management limitations.

The design of Policy Governance enables a board to make its decisions at the broadest of levels first, leveraging all other company decisions through these few controlling policy statements. At the broadest levels of policy it is perfectly possible for a board to know what it wants and does not want. The board does not have to have a lot of information about how to make a widget or how to operate a factory. The board does have to decide what making widgets and operating factories are *for* and what risks it wants the company to avoid along the way. To make those kinds of decisions, the board needs to know what is happening outside the company as much as what is going on inside. Board competence in Policy Governance is not about mirroring management competence. It is about setting and monitoring the framework within which management's competence is exercised. Boards certainly require information, but information for their own purposes, as we shall explain in the next chapter.

Creating Ends Policies

Framing ends may well be the most challenging job for a board. Once the ends have been fixed, assuming that the board has chosen to look to the long term, they may remain fairly stable for a few years.

However, it is still essential for the board to routinely monitor the CEO's fulfillment of the ends and regularly review the assumptions on which it made its decisions.

Boards tend to have a greater variety of expectations about desirable ends than they do about unacceptable means. Therefore the chances that our samples of Ends policies will be directly relevant to a particular company are lower than they are for our other samples. Nevertheless, they are still likely to be useful templates. (The two Ends policies presented in this chapter are especially relevant to publicly traded companies. Appendix E also offers sample Ends policies for a family company, a start-up owned by two persons, and a company with a single owner.)

Each of our examples (Exhibits 5.1 and 5.2), "Shareholder Value" [Version 1] and "Shareholder Value" [Version 2], starts of course at the broadest level. The two boards writing these policies clearly have different views about what owner value should be. A few moments' reflection on the different CEO actions required to fulfill each of these policies gives an idea of the powerful leverage that can come from a few brief words of policy.

It is typical that corporate boards have far less to say in their Ends policies than in the other categories. (Nonprofit and governmental boards, however, ordinarily have much more to say in their Ends policies than do corporate boards.) Figure 5.1 illustrates the Ends category completed at a fairly typical level of detail.

Exhibit 5.1. Ends Policy "Shareholder Value" [Version 1].

The ultimate aim of the company is economic benefit to shareholders.

1. The company shall achieve ___% compounded growth in annual earnings per share by [*year*] and thereafter.
    A. By the end of [*that year minus 3*] performance will be at least ___%.
    B. By the end of [*that year minus 1*] performance will be at least ___%.

Exhibit 5.2. Ends Policy "Shareholder Value" [Version 2].

The ultimate aim of the company is return on shareholder equity better than the return for firms of similar risk characteristics.

1. Risk characteristics for comparison will include similar size, industry, and maturity of market.
2. Better return will mean above the median for such firms, rather than above the average.

Mission Statements and Strategic Plans

We must add a word here about the mission statements and strategic plans that many corporations have developed. Mission statements are written in a number of formats, usually by management. Many are inspiring, many are rhetorically pleasing; all require an investment of time and thoughtfulness. One might wonder whether the shorter form of mission statement differs in any way from the global, or broadest, expression of Ends. In fact, the two may not be related at all! Rarely do common mission statements conform to the results recipients worth formula that sets Ends policies apart from normal goal setting. The need for Ends policy to be bare-bones and stark in its clarity will usually preclude its use as an inspiring mission statement.

In other words, company mission statements as ordinarily conceived and written have little or nothing to do with governance and much to do with management. The board's obligation to owners is to ensure that management knows—and is routinely judged against—just what owner value is to be produced; the board is not obligated to generate an inspiring statement to include in brochures and annual reports or to decorate office walls. Management is perfectly capable of producing inspiring and beautiful statements, and probably has been the source of them all along anyway. A mission statement written by management to influence employees and customers is undoubtedly a good idea, but it neither duplicates the board's Ends

Figure 5.1. Ends Policies Completed.

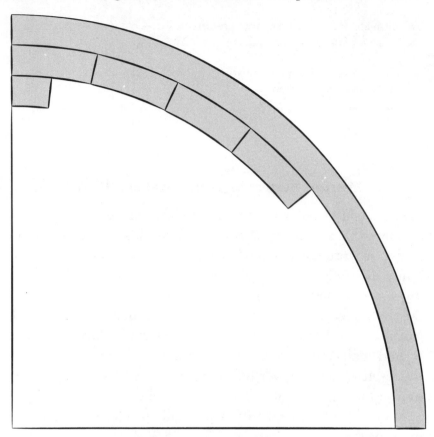

The board has established its Ends policies deeply enough that any decisions or choices made by a delegatee will be acceptable to the board if they are a reasonable interpretation of the broader statements. Thus the board can now safely delegate all further decisions in this category. It is likely that the board of a company will need no more than two levels of depth in these policies.

nor relieves the board from its task of stating those Ends in unvarnished language. The Policy Governance solution, then, is to leave mission writing to management, while the board goes about its unadorned, company-driving, performance-demanding ends task.

The approval of strategic plans is another common way for boards to involve themselves in goal setting. The content of strategic plans, however, generally relates primarily to means, and whatever ends components are included are usually obscure and imprecise. In other words, strategic plans are not governance documents, because they usually say not enough about what the company is for and very much about what the company is to do. Boards that approve strategic plans are merely approving management's means choices rather than defining what the choices should achieve and then allowing management to use its skills, knowledge, and talent to make the choices as it sees fit.

Creating Management Limitations Policies

Management Limitations is the policy category within which the board can say whatever it has to say about cash flow, budgeting, compliance with legal and regulatory authority requirements, treatment of customers, employee issues, alliances, care of the environment, and any other areas in which things might go wrong or be otherwise unacceptable. As in all policymaking, it is vital that the board stick to the design discipline of starting with the broadest level first—for the sake of both including all that needs to be included and saying no more than needs to be said. Notice in the following examples how addressing the larger values that lie behind decisions clarifies the key issues and produces very clear instructions with a minimum of words.

The initial global, all-embracing Management Limitations sample statement (Exhibit 5.3), "Basic Executive Constraints," captures at the broadest level *everything* that the board might want to prohibit. The effect is that at least at the broad level, there is no management means issue over which the board has not at this point established control. The board then goes on to further define its global prohibition and, "without limiting the scope of the [global prohibition] by this enumeration," to address a few issues in more detail. It thus goes on to specifically rule out some of the interpretation range the CEO would have had if the board stopped with the global policy level. According to the rule we have already explained, at whatever level in its policies the board stops speaking,

Exhibit 5.3. Management Limitations Policy "Basic Executive Constraints."

The CEO shall not cause or allow any practice, activity, decision, or organizational circumstance that is unlawful, imprudent, or in violation of generally accepted business and professional ethics or generally accepted accounting principles.

Further, without limiting the scope of the foregoing by this enumeration:

1. **Treatment of Stakeholders.** With respect to interactions with business partners, regulators, vendors, the local community, and the environment, the CEO shall not cause or allow conditions, procedures, or decisions that are unsafe, undignified, or unnecessarily intrusive.

2. **Treatment of Employees.** With respect to the treatment of employees, the CEO may not cause or allow conditions that are unsafe, unfair, or undignified.

3. **Financial Planning and Budgeting.** Financial planning for any fiscal year or the remaining part of any fiscal year shall not risk fiscal jeopardy, fail to be derived from a multiyear plan, or fail to be consistent with the company performance under other Management Limitations and Ends policies.

4. **Financial Conditions and Activities.** With respect to actual, ongoing financial conditions and activities, the CEO shall not cause or allow the development of fiscal jeopardy, compromised fiduciary responsibility, or material deviation from the board's Ends policies.

5. **Emergency Loss of CEO.** The CEO shall not fail to protect the company from loss of its CEO.

6. **Asset Protection.** The CEO shall not allow corporate assets to be unprotected, inadequately maintained, or unnecessarily risked.

7. **Investments.** The CEO shall not fail to invest excess corporate funds to maximize after-tax interest income but in so doing shall not risk loss of principal or maintenance of proper liquidity.

8. **Compensation and Benefits.** With respect to employment, compensation, and benefits of employees, consultants, and contract workers, the CEO shall not cause or allow short-term or long-term jeopardy to fiscal integrity or to company image.

9. **Communication to and Support of the Board.** The CEO shall not permit the board to be uninformed or unsupported in its work.

10. **Trading in Company Securities.** The CEO shall not allow management personnel to trade in company securities under a less stringent code of integrity than the board has adopted for itself.

11. **Diversification.** The CEO shall not risk the company's future by failure to diversify.

12. **Dealings with Shareholders.** The CEO's relationship with shareholders shall neither violate the highest standards of transparency and responsiveness nor impede the board's role as shareholder representative.

the CEO acquires the freedom to make *any* reasonable interpretation of the board's words.

The board might then proceed to a further level of specificity for one or more of the second-level statements in this "Basic Executive Constraints" policy, again without limiting the scope of the broader statements. The policies "Financial Conditions and Activities" (Exhibit 5.4) and "Communication to and Support of the Board" (Exhibit 5.5) offer samples of this procession into greater detail. (The Management Limitations samples in Appendix E cover such topics as asset protection; trading in company securities; diversification; and treatment of shareholders, staff, and other stakeholders. We have found these policies widely applicable among boards, but inevitably and quite rightly each board will have its own versions.)

Financial Condition and Activities

The ongoing financial situation and actions of a company are among the board's topmost concerns. To gain a sense of control over this crucial area, boards typically rely on relatively standard financial reports, containing mainly historical data and submitted by or under the authority of the CEO. In the Policy Governance framework, the board thinks through and states ahead of time the financial situations or actions that would be unacceptable. All the myriad financial actions and variations normal to the business that do not violate these boundaries are, by definition, acceptable and unremarkable. The board expresses these limits of financial acceptability in its Management Limitations policies, including, for example, the one shown in Exhibit 5.4.

Exhibit 5.4. Management Limitations Policy "Financial Conditions and Activities."

With respect to actual, ongoing financial condition and activities, the CEO shall not cause or allow the development of fiscal jeopardy, compromised fiduciary responsibility, or material deviation from the board's Ends policies.

Further, without limiting the scope of the foregoing by this enumeration, he or she shall not

1. Maintain reserve accounts for the purposes of managing earnings to meet market expectations or for other questionable purposes.
2. Operate the company so as to cause it to be in default under any of its financial agreements.
3. Fail to follow [applicable accounting standards] in the maintenance of the financial records of the company.
4. Fail to settle payroll and debts in a timely manner.
5. Allow tax payments or other government-ordered payments or filings to be overdue or inaccurately filed.
6. Make a single purchase or commitment of greater than [*money amount*]. Splitting orders to avoid this limit is not acceptable.
7. Fail to aggressively pursue receivables after a reasonable grace period.

A board might further decide that the provisions of this "Financial Conditions and Activities" policy are insufficient. Even bearing in mind that financial management must also meet the broadly stated requirements of the global Management Limitations policy (Exhibit 5.3), the board might choose to go into yet more detail, tailoring the policy to the company's specific circumstances and perceived jeopardy.

Communication to and Support of the Board

The "Communication to and Support of the Board" policy (Exhibit 5.5) announces it is unacceptable for management to provide insufficient information and support for board work. Information, the policy clarifies, includes data that measure policy compliance, facts that forewarn the board of anticipated noncompliance,

Exhibit 5.5. Management Limitations Policy
"Communication to and Support of the Board."

The CEO shall not permit the board to be uninformed or unsupported in its work.

Further, without limiting the scope of the foregoing by this enumeration, he or she shall not

1. Neglect to submit monitoring data required by the board in a timely, accurate, and understandable manner (see the "Monitoring CEO Performance" policy), directly addressing the provisions of the board policies being monitored.

2. Fail to report in a timely manner an actual or anticipated noncompliance with any board policy.

3. Let the board be unaware of relevant trends, anticipated adverse media coverage, threatened or pending lawsuits, backgrounds of all key management personnel, significant issues with major business partners, and material external and internal changes, particularly changes in the assumptions on which any board policy has previously been established.

4. Fail to advise the board if, in the CEO's opinion, the board is not in compliance with its own policies on Governance Process and Board Management Delegation, particularly in the case of board behavior detrimental to the relationship between the board and the CEO.

5. Fail to marshal for the board as many management and external points of view, issues, and options as the board determines it needs for fully informed board choices.

6. Present information in an unnecessarily complex or lengthy form or in a form that fails to differentiate among information of three types: monitoring, decision preparation, and other.

7. Fail to provide a mechanism for board and committee meetings; for official board, officer, or committee communications; for maintenance of accurate board and director records; and for board disclosures required by law or deemed appropriate by the board.

8. Selectively disclose corporate information to individual directors or investors, with the exception of responding to officers or committees duly charged by the board.

9. Fail to supply the CEO's decisions along with applicable monitoring data for the board's consent agenda in respect to decisions delegated to the CEO yet required by law or contract to be board approved.

knowledge of developments that could affect the company adversely, and any other data that might cause the board to reexamine its policies. Support includes the mechanical and logistical aids needed by any board as it goes about its task.

Whereas the policy depicted in Exhibit 5.3 fits in the outer two levels of the policy circle (approximately as in Figure 5.2), when all Management Limitations policies are complete, a visual display will approximate Figure 5.3.

Figure 5.2. Management Limitations Policies: Levels One and Two.

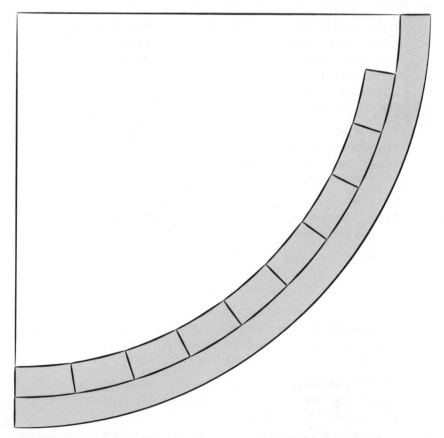

The board has created the global level and one further level of detail in its Management Limitations policies. With policy language taken to the second level, the global proscription of certain management means has been extended into such specific areas as asset protection, budgeting, and treatment of employees.

Interpretation of Ends and Management Limitations Policies

Because the Ends and Management Limitations policy categories govern CEO and all other management action, the power of reasonable interpretation belongs to the CEO—an authority explicitly set down in a Board-Management Delegation policy (Exhibit 4.1). So once the board has made Ends and Management Limitations decisions in whatever detail it wishes, the CEO is authorized to

Figure 5.3. Management Limitations Policies Completed.

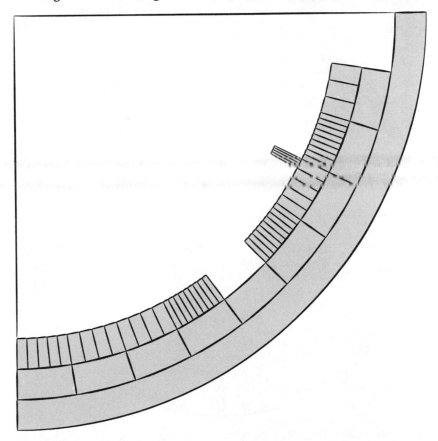

The completed Management Limitations policies cover all possible board worries about management means because they begin at the broadest level (covering everything) and extend to the desired level of specificity. At this point the board feels it is safe to say that the CEO is automatically authorized to make any management means decisions not prohibited in these policies.

make all further decisions on these topics, as long as those decisions are a reasonable interpretation of the board's words.

Domains of CEO and Chair Decision Authority

Figure 5.4 approximates what the completed policy circle might look like. The board has done its work in each policy quadrant at the broadest level and in whatever level of detail it has chosen. Nor-

**Figure 5.4. Sample Profile of Board Policies
Completed in All Four Categories.**

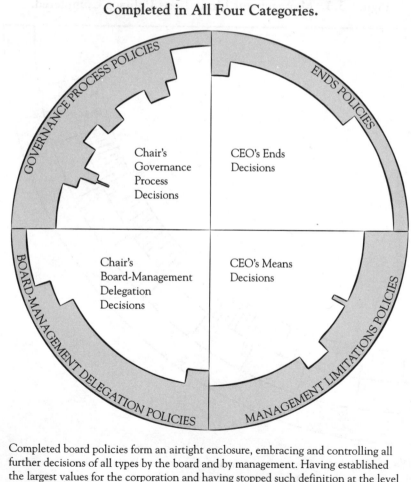

Completed board policies form an airtight enclosure, embracing and controlling all further decisions of all types by the board and by management. Having established the largest values for the corporation and having stopped such definition at the level where it will permit any reasonable interpretation, the board has defined the domains of the board and its chair on the one hand and the CEO on the other. The board retains the right to change policy content and depth.

mally, a board's policy manual will be about the length of the set of sample policies in Appendix E. Each policy should be coded with its category, the date adopted, and the dates of any amendments.

We have explained in the previous two chapters that the chair is authorized to interpret the board's words and take further action under Governance Process and Board-Management Delegation policies. In this chapter, we have said that the CEO is authorized to interpret the board's words and take further action under Ends and Management Limitations policies.

The visual depiction shows that this division of authority results in separate domains for the chair and CEO, in which they each make decisions—always of course within a reasonable interpretation of the applicable board policies. Chair and CEO are not hierarchically related jobs, but they are adjacent jobs, each with a distinct and important role to play. The CEO has no authority or responsibility on the left side of the circle. The chair has no authority or responsibility on the right side.

Looking Back, Moving Forward

This chapter has described how the board can drive company performance by defining its expectations of the CEO. These expectations take the form of the ends the board requires to be accomplished and the limits the board places on the means choices and conditions available to the CEO. In the next chapter we discuss how the board can ensure that its policies are actually being put into practice.

Chapter Six

Reporting Board and Management Performance

What you cannot enforce, do not command.

—*Sophocles*[1]

In This Chapter

- Why too much information can be worse than none
- Reporting for the future and reporting for the past
- Creating performance monitoring reports
- Evaluating the CEO

The Policy Governance model enables a board to drive company performance by means of succinctly crafted policies that both maintain the board's own discipline and instruct the CEO. In the comprehensive policy system of Policy Governance, these policies embody all the board's decisions. Because the board's job is about translating owners' wishes into company performance, proper governance requires accountability of the CEO to the board then accountability of the board to owners. Reporting is the mechanism through which the information necessary for that accountability is collected and conveyed.

Governance Information Issues

Information for governance presents problems for boards, for CEOs, and ultimately for owners. Most vexing are the problems of how to deal with the sheer volume of information, how to use different kinds of information appropriately, and how to get information from external as well as internal sources.

Information Overload

There is probably no governance function with which boards have more familiarity than reporting. Reporting usually takes the form of quantities of material sent out to directors in advance of their meetings and in-person executive presentations at the meetings. The amount of time spent absorbing information prior to and during board meetings can be far greater than the time spent in debate during the meetings. And reviewing the past always threatens to use up time needed to deliberate and to design expectations for the future. Given a board's limited time and energy it is important that directors' attention be focused on the right issues and used efficiently.

Focusing on the right issues is much harder when the board has too much information. Yet because the board is accountable for everything that a company is and does, the board is potentially interested in everything. In practice, the information that the board receives is filtered through senior management, so that it arrives at the board table by the folder rather than the truckload. The downside of this arrangement is that in the absence of precise instructions from the board, the CEO becomes the judge of what deserves to be reported. Even the most scrupulous and conscientious CEO can be open to accusations of manipulation and information control, and the very best of boards can be criticized for subservience to management's control of information.

When they are not able to specify precisely what information they require, some boards ask to see far more than they can realistically digest. Indeed, some CEOs provide more than directors can realistically digest, whether or not they have been asked to do so. When directors have too much information, they may enjoy a sense of security, but it is a false sense, for, bedazzled or buried, they fail to recognize what they still don't have. Moreover, important information can be diluted or even completely drowned out by information overload. The sense of not knowing what is really going on is a common fear. But until it learns how to distinguish what it really needs to know, a board will find it hard to strike a satisfactory balance between too much information and too little.

Information Use

It can also be unclear to a board what it should do with the information it gets. As a result, one common practice is for directors to read or listen using their own expertise and experience as a filter, pick out the bits that seem important, ask whatever questions occur to them, and then offer their opinion or advice. If debate stops there, the CEO has heard a range of opinions from a range of directors and leaves the meeting with some words of experienced counsel. However, the CEO may be unsure about the extent to which he or she is obliged to act on the advice, and directors may be uncertain whether they have covered everything important. It is not uncommon in such a scenario for directors to have participated in a management decision—and to have done it well—yet to have done no governance work at all.

On a brighter note, we suspect that recent years have seen an improvement in presenting information to boards clearly marked, when applicable, as calling for a decision. We now wish to take this trend further.

Information Source

Suppose then that the board is fully aware that it should make a decision on a CEO request (and that this decision really should be made by the board and is not an instance of the approval syndrome discussed in Chapter Five). The board then reads or listens to senior management's presentation of the question, examines the various directors' opinions, and finds a majority opinion. A problem in this scenario is that the board is reacting exclusively to information from the CEO, rather than reaching out to gather information from a variety of sources including owners and expert advisers. If the board is making big decisions about what the company is for or about sources of substantial risk, it needs not only a certain amount of inside information but as much or more information from the environment in which the company operates. Management opinion, as important as it is, must not be the board's only information source if governance is to be credible to owners.

Classes of Governance Information

The design of Policy Governance takes account of the fact that to fulfill the total governance job the board needs information, first, to help it create policies and, second, to monitor them. More than any other organizational position, the board works almost entirely with information. It manufactures nothing; it sells nothing; it builds nothing. It considers information and makes decisions about it. The board's purpose for gathering information is not to satisfy idle curiosity or suspicion but to gain knowledge, wisdom, assurance, and forewarning. Policy Governance distinguishes classes of information based on a board's use of the information. Directors are accustomed to thinking about reporting as information about the topic under scrutiny—for instance, product development or capital planning. Policy Governance requires that directors think first in terms of the purpose to which reported information will be put.

Boards have two distinct official uses for information. First, they need *decision information*, information that enables them to make decisions. Second, they need *performance information*, data that enable them to know whether the company is meeting expectations the board has established in its Ends and Management Limitations policies. The first prepares the board to determine the future. The second permits the board to judge the past. These two types of information are the only ones needed for governing.

Yet board members are of course human beings with wide interests and curiosity. There are other things they would like to know—information that goes beyond what they need to carry out their governing responsibility. We call this *incidental information*, not to disparage it but to recognize that it is optional as far as the board's job is concerned.

In traditional governance these three types of information tend to be mingled together without regard for their very different uses. Hence financial information presented to the board may contain, first, information that discloses whether a previous board demand for, say, a minimum level of liquidity has been met; second, information that supplies the understanding needed for board action on, say, a dividend declaration under consideration; and third, information that does neither of these things but is of personal interest to one or more directors or to no one.

For the sake of clarity, focus, and efficiency, information reported to the board should be divided into categories of *decision making*, *performance monitoring*, and *incidental*. It is easy to underestimate the power of this simple categorization and even easier to fail to follow it with rigor. Boards need to ensure that information comes to them with its category clearly marked (with any device that works for the board). Directors can then easily see whether they have the decision information they need for a decision or sufficient performance information to know whether the CEO is doing his or her job. They can also indulge in incidental information for interest's sake once they are absolutely certain their official obligations are being fulfilled.

Decision Information: Information for Demanding Future Accomplishments

In the Policy Governance framework, with its nested bowl design and four exhaustive subject areas, all decisions facing the board fall into the policy categories of Governance Process, Board-Management Delegation, Ends, and Management Limitations. When the board gathers wisdom for making decisions, these areas are what the decisions are about.

Because the board's work is to decide and demand rather than to poke and probe, its decision making is at the front end of the corporate parade. To make these leadership decisions wisely the board needs to get information from whatever sources it finds sufficiently authoritative, accurate, and economical. Information can come from management, from the market, from owners, from expert advisers, and from directors' experience.

Information to Decide Ends Policies. Many boards have enough experienced directors for a respectable debate on ends with no outside input. But this apparent self-sufficiency can be deceptive. The board should use at least the same level of appropriate input in specifying ends as it does in, say, containing risk. It is essential that the board be able to give the CEO carefully considered and specific instructions and therefore drive company performance wisely on this most important of corporate topics.

Owner Input. Although the board, morally and legally, can exercise a great deal of discretion in its choice of desired ends, directors must go beyond their personal experiences and philosophies of corporate value creation to attain the level of wisdom required to make such decisions. Because different shareholders desire different values, the board needs to *know* shareholders, in whatever sense is reasonable—obviously, large public company boards cannot be on familiar terms with owners in the same way or to the same extent as the directors of a closely held company can.

Generally, boards are legally obliged to afford all shareholders the same basic rights, but majority shareholders and particular classes of shareholders have more voting power than others at general shareholder meetings. At board meetings every director's voting power is equal, and every director is equally obliged to act in the interests of all shareholders. However, it is easy to see (especially as some board members might represent the most significant shareholders) how in practice a board might overlook the interests of minority owners. Each board needs to consider and come to defensible conclusions about the extent to which minority shareholders' interests can reasonably be assumed to be the same as all other shareholders' interests. To the extent to which the board has an ethical belief that minority interests need special protection, it should set relevant standards for itself in the Governance Process policies.

The board's relationship with shareholders is not one of public relations so much as one of input and accountability. The CEO's relationship with owners is not one of input and accountability (though it can be one of public relations and delegated responsibility from the board for the logistical, informational, and other mechanics required to maintain the company's investor relations), with one exception. Management could also be charged (perhaps in the "Communication to and Support of the Board" policy, shown in Exhibit 5.5) with the *mechanics* of gathering or arranging shareholder polling, interviewing, or surveying.

Environmental Input. In addition to learning the characteristics and expressed needs of owners, the board must keep informed of certain changes in the wider environment. For example, what is the profitability of other companies in the same business? How broadly should that reference group be defined? What industry or competitive changes are likely to alter those findings, and over what time period? What environmental or company changes would cause the board to alter the rolling average period it previously chose for a shareholder value measure? What political or social changes that could affect the company are in the pipeline?

Expert Input. The board should be aware of any emerging calculus of owner value that might enable it to better capture the meaning of the value it favors. Different definitions are being developed all the time along with new terminology. Already boards and companies can use measures such as WACC (weighted average cost of capital) and EVA (economic value added), SVA (shareholder value added), and CFROI (cash flow return on investment), and by the time this book is published, there will be still more. The level of debate is clearly far beyond the elementary *share price versus profit* argument. The meaning of *bottom line* is not nearly so straightforward as it first appears. Directors must become experts in this matter, so they can competently express the core reasons for corporate existence, as representatives of the voice of the owners.

Management Input. Management's input can be valuable as part of any of the previous inputs; however, it is particularly required for assessing the feasibility of Ends policies. Decisions about the future should not be limited by the past or even the current state of the company's affairs yet must clearly take past and present into account. The Ends policies need to paint a clear target for the CEO, to be achieved within whatever time frame the board decides, and that target has to be credible as well as desirable.

The board may ask anyone it wishes, including the CEO, to help it get any of the information it needs, but it must always remember that it, not the CEO or anyone else, is accountable to owners for ensuring that its decisions are based on sufficient and credible information.

Information to Decide Management Limitations Policies. The information that the board needs to decide on Management Limitations policies does not require directors to know everything about the company. However, it does require them to be able to identify all their proper concerns about possible company means and to know what limitations on those means it is realistic to require. This information generally comes from a combination of directors' previous experience, senior management input, expert advice, and general industry standards.

As we noted in Chapter Five, when it comes to concerns about the CEO's means, there is a great deal of similarity among boards. Every board is concerned about protecting assets, debt, public image, and so on. Every board worries about sources of jeopardy; every board wishes to demand probity and ethics. Therefore the templates that appear in Appendix E are a good place for any board to start, allowing the board to avoid reinventing the wheel. However, every board must also make the policies its own through thorough consideration and appropriate adjustment. For example, it may be wise for one board to restrain risks of diversification (adopting a *stick to your knitting* strategy), for another board it may be wise to prohibit the risks of having a single, albeit successful, product (adopting a *don't put all your eggs in one basket* strategy).

Information to Decide Governance Process Policies. To decide on its Governance Process policies, the directors need to seek information about what constitutes good governance from relevant authorities, from the best available thinking of academics and practitioners, and from each other. The board's decisions in this category will become the measures of the board's own behavior and the behavior of its committees and chair. The board needs to decide on its size, its election methodology, its code of conduct, the desirable mix of directors, how it wishes to safeguard both management freedom and governance wholeness, how it will employ self-evaluation, and so on.

Information to Decide Board-Management Delegation Policies. To decide on the policies that describe the official relationship between the board and management, the board must be clear about what it means by and wants from the CEO function. It needs to decide the way in which it wishes to monitor and evaluate performance, the frequency of that monitoring and evaluation, the way it will handle suspected or informally reported violations of policy, and so on. These are decisions of principle and common sense for which the necessary information lies pretty much entirely within the boardroom itself.

Performance Information: Information for Judging the Past

Most reporting is about the past. The board can react, but it cannot change the reality that performance information reports present. For example, although the audit and the audit committee perform a vital function in examining financial data, these data record the past. But in the same way that making sure the rules were not violated is not the point of a game, reviewing the past is not the prime purpose of a board. Information about the past is indispensable when the board is evaluating the company and its CEO. But even excellent financial numbers mean that someone made good decisions in the past, not that today's decisions—the only ones the board can affect—are good.

However, recognizing the shortcomings of historical information does not make it unimportant. Accountability is impossible without it. When the board fails to verify whether its Ends policies have been fulfilled and whether its Management Limitations policies have been observed, it sends a message that these policies do not matter. The links between these policies and monitoring are simply these: first, performance monitoring is done *only* on the content of these policies and, second, *no* components of these policies should escape monitoring. Policymaking and performance monitoring are thus inextricably linked.

Gathering information about company performance should not mean hunting about in lengthy reports. With the design of Policy Governance, the board knows exactly what it needs to gain from performance information. It needs to know no more and no less than the amount and kind of information necessary to reveal the degree of compliance with any reasonable interpretation of its policies. More than enough information clutters a report and dilutes its utility, obscuring data specific to the criteria addressed. Less than enough fails to satisfy directors' need for assurance that their stated expectations are being met.

As to assessing the performance of the board itself, including the performance of its committees and chair, the only criteria to be monitored appear in the board's Governance Process and Board-Management Delegation policies. As the board codifies company performance expectations in policies and expects the CEO to perform upon them, it codifies board performance in policies and expects itself, its committees, and its chair to perform upon them. In both cases the board must assess how well the policies are being fulfilled.

Incidental Information

Incidental information can take any form the board chooses as long as it is clearly demarcated from the decision and performance monitoring information, which is truly needed to govern. The board may choose to use separate tabs in the meeting book, different color paper, presentations to the board that are outside the official board meeting, or whatever else works for it.

It is not impossible that a board might come across something in incidental information that triggers a policy review, but this happenstance can never substitute for rigorous, criteria-focused data on performance. Directors' time spent on considering incidental information is almost always time not spent on governance. Incidental information is just that—nice to know but inessential.

Creating the Monitoring System

This section focuses on the monitoring of CEO performance. For convenience, we use the term *performance monitoring* to mean assessment of the management (hence of the CEO). However, the board's performance must also be assessed, and we deal with the board's *self-evaluation* in the next chapter.

The Monitoring Schedule

The first task in performance monitoring is to create a monitoring schedule. For the monitoring of CEO, and therefore management, performance the board will monitor every policy in the Ends category and in the Management Limitations category. For each policy, the board decides on a method and frequency of monitoring. Like all board decisions, these are recorded in policy too (see Exhibit 4.3, "Monitoring CEO Performance"). In choosing a method, the board decides whether it will receive monitoring data from the CEO (the most common source), from an external source (such as an auditor), or from its own direct inspection (Exhibit 6.1).

To monitor the global Ends policy statement, the board need only ask for reports on the lower level statements, because together these should constitute the board's definition of its Ends. To monitor the global Management Limitations policy, however, the board may want to add an occasional random check (through direct board inspection or external report) of risk areas encompassed by the global policy prohibition that have not been further specified in lower level policy.

Management should play no role in external reporting other than to cooperate. For reporting to qualify as external, the reporter must be *completely* under the control of the board. If an auditing firm, for example, even *perceives* that management influences, much less controls, its selection and continued service, the independence required for high standard external monitoring is sullied.

Monitoring Frequency

The frequency of monitoring can be whatever the board finds appropriate, ordinarily any period from monthly to annually. The policies that govern areas the board considers especially sensitive or especially subject to change should be monitored with the great-

Exhibit 6.1. Performance Monitoring Methods.

- **CEO report:** data disclosing performance on the provisions of a policy, gathered by the CEO or the CEO's subordinates and attested to by the CEO
- **External inspection:** data disclosing performance on the provisions of a policy, gathered by and attested to by an outside, disinterested party, such as an auditor
- **Board inspection:** data disclosing performance on the provisions of a policy, gathered by the board or an assigned organ of the board, such as an officer or committee

est frequency. Whatever the frequency set by the board for routine monitoring, the board retains the right to monitor any policy anytime it chooses.

Monitoring Report Format

When the CEO delivers a performance monitoring report to the board in accord with board policy, the construction of the report is important. We suggest that monitoring reports should contain the following three features: first, the report reiterates the provisions of the policy being monitored (saving directors from having to look up the policy). Second, the report sets down the interpretation the CEO has made of each policy provision and anything that the CEO wishes to say to support the reasonableness of that interpretation. Third, the report cites data that demonstrate compliance with that interpretation of the policy.

The board need not involve itself in the design of reporting forms, for that engages directors in an unnecessary level of detail. Governance is quite well served if the board merely receives reports and judges whether it is convinced, sending the CEO back to the drawing board if it is not. In other words, the directors' friendly but firm attitude is "prove it to us."

The same principle applies when the board is receiving reports from an external audit or inspection. Although financial audits follow conventions set by specialists beyond the board, the board must demand control over what it needs to learn from the audit or any other report. This call for assertiveness has implications for the demands a responsible board must make of its auditors for independence, thoroughness, and pointed replies to policy-based monitoring questions.

Reasonable Proof

Proper monitoring does not consist of the CEO's simply giving his or her assurance (the "trust me" method). Objective data must be provided that the board can accept as reasonable proof that its policy has been complied with. *Reasonable proof* is proof that can be produced given a reasonable expenditure of time and financial resources. Sound data can be produced about pretty much anything if you have unlimited time and money. The reality, however, is that there is a point at which the cost of gathering information is greater than the value of producing it. Ultimately this judgment call belongs to the board, not to the CEO.

Components of a CEO Report

Exhibit 6.2 shows a portion of a CEO monitoring report (the full report appears in Appendix F). Note that it is constructed around the three components described previously. The CEO always gives his or her interpretation of the policy being monitored, but lets the board know whether it is the same interpretation the board has seen in previous reports. If an interpretation was acceptable before, it likely still is. Where board policy has not been successfully implemented, the CEO's notation clearly shows that failure. (Remember that such noncompliance should already have been reported under the second subsection of the board's "Communication to and Support of the Board" policy, as shown in Exhibit 5.5.)

Board Processing of Monitoring Reports

The monitoring schedule controls when monitoring reports are due to the board. Generally, directors have these reports circulated to them in writing before board meetings. At the meeting, each director, in showing due care, confirms that he or she has received, read, and been satisfied or not satisfied with each report's representation of performance. When a majority of directors believe that performance on a reasonable interpretation of a particular policy has not been proven, then the board must discuss the matter and decide the proper response. This response could be anything from asking the CEO to submit a more convincing report to changing the pol-

Exhibit 6.2. Excerpt from CEO Monitoring Report.

Monitoring Board Policy "Asset Protection"

POLICY PROVISION 2
The CEO shall not allow unbonded personnel access to material amounts of funds.

CEO's Interpretation
[ITALIZED SECTION CHANGED SINCE LAST REPORT] "Unbonded personnel" is interpreted to mean employees who are refused inclusion in the organization's insurance against employee wrongdoing. "Material" is interpreted to mean any amount over $500 per access *or $5,000 cumulatively in a twelve-month period*. This interpretation was based on advice received from the organization's auditor as well as the National Association of Organizations Like Ours. Personnel who have "access" is interpreted to mean those who, due to the course of their duties, should be included in the insurance against employee wrongdoing. "Funds" means not only the amounts mentioned above but also items convertible to funds, including the organization's checks, check signing machine, petty cash, and purchase order forms.

Data
A review of our insurance covering employee wrongdoing shows that all employees who have access as defined are listed. Procedures are in place that protect access to petty cash, checks, signing machines, and purchase order forms. A spot check conducted in the last week demonstrated that in all cases, no access can be obtained by unauthorized persons and that no access is possible without the knowledge of two key holders.

I report compliance.

icy itself to issuing a reprimand or even to terminating the CEO, depending on the type and extent of performance deficit.

Evaluating the CEO

The logic of CEO evaluation in Policy Governance is this: the board's only requirements for management performance are expressed in Ends policies and in Management Limitations policies. The CEO is held personally accountable for management performance and only that performance. It is as though the board does not evaluate the CEO at all. It evaluates the entire management performance and attributes it to the CEO. The performance monitoring system is a continual reading of Ends achievement and Management Limitations compliance. Therefore the regular monitoring revelations *are* the CEO's evaluation.

Annual or other periodic CEO evaluation is an accumulation of all the monitoring reports received throughout the previous period, no more, no less. *No more* because to add other judgments at this point implies the board was not serious in stating that all criteria are contained in the policies. *No less* because to omit some policies means the board did not intend them to be taken seriously. Given the thoroughness of the performance monitoring system, formal evaluation represents a momentary punctuation of a continuous process. In effect on future company performance, the punctuation is not nearly so important as that which it punctuates. Sporadic measurement is not nearly so powerful in shaping behavior as continual feedback.

Changing circumstances can of course lead the board to alter its policies and therefore its expectations. There is no merit in expecting the undoable. This possibility of amendment does not change the fact that at any given moment the performance criteria are fixed. But the formal evaluation is an opportunity for the board to take extraordinary situations into account. Yes, the expectations were not met; that is sheer fact. But, no, the board does not think ill of the CEO given the market, civil, political, or economic circumstances that transpired. We suggest that the monitoring system show unvarnished fact. It is in the periodic evaluation that the board can introduce sympathy if, at that time and in its judgment, such leniency best serves owners' interests.

We do not pretend that such a judgment call by a board is easy. The concept of accountability is so critical in corporate affairs that letting anyone off the hook for performance may precipitate the collapse of the concept. The highway speed laws are not changed when a person is caught speeding, however good his or her reasons for driving too fast. Yet it would be ludicrous for boards to fire U.S. airline CEOs for losses due to the September 2001 terrorist attacks. We offer no answer except that directors must apply conscientiousness and wisdom in the context of their commitment to what is best for owners.

CEO compensation is also a topic of great importance and wide interest and is studied by many experts. We do not presume to have new answers for this complicated subject. We can, however, make several pronouncements drawn from the Policy Governance model. First, CEO compensation must be linked in some justifiable way to management performance, that is, to the monitoring and evaluation we have just discussed. Second, CEO compensation should be set by a board of impeccable independence, its judgment driven by market rather than internal influences. Third, the board's values as they relate to CEO compensation should be set forth in a Board-Management Delegation policy that the board or a board compensation committee must adhere to when making actual compensation decisions.

Monitoring and Transparency

The transparency of a company's affairs to its owners is a topic that resurfaces every time a major company runs into trouble. We can not resist the urge to suggest that Policy Governance provides directors and owners with a tremendous opportunity in this respect. A board that can command and account for company performance as clearly as Policy Governance boards can must surely provide investors and regulators alike with a degree of security that other boards would struggle to emulate.

Looking Back, Moving Forward

This chapter has outlined how the board gathers information to make policy decisions and how the board ensures accountability for company performance through monitoring the CEO's implementation of board policies. In the next chapter we turn to examining the way the board can ensure the continuing adequacy of its own performance in light of its policies for itself.

Chapter Seven

Maintaining the Gains

The degree to which corporations observe basic
principles of good corporate governance is an
increasingly important factor in investment decisions.
—*Organization for Economic Cooperation and Development*[1]

In This Chapter

- Keeping the board on track with Policy Governance
- Conducting board meetings in which the board does its job
- Asking three questions: a critical discipline
- Surviving dangerous moments
- Evaluating the board

The last chapter examined the types of information the board needs. This chapter discusses the discipline required to continue to do the board job with excellence. In order to govern a company successfully a board must first successfully govern itself.

The board's Governance Process policies constitute a stable template for board behavior that can serve through good times, tricky times, and bad times. The board's job is constant and Governance Process policies (as amended from time to time) are the board's instruments for navigating a constant course. Discipline is required to use the policies consistently and properly. Like real navigational instruments, these instruments cannot help if they are ignored or not maintained or even abandoned in a crisis—the very time they are most needed.

Sustaining Commitment

Initial enthusiasm for a new approach provides motivation for only a limited time. Old habits die hard and resurface easily. Time-honored board practices can feel like safety, even when they cloak a perilous state. The Policy Governance framework provides a carefully designed way for the board to control its company, but its unfamiliarity can cause even committed directors to feel uncertain.

Moreover, Policy Governance requires new skills and uncommon integrity with language. It also calls for a good deal of commitment to a deliberate process in the face of crises or other provocations to engage in either overcontrol or undercontrol. It also requires strong board leadership on behalf of owners in the same way that it requires strong CEO leadership on behalf of the board.

The concepts, principles, and formats of Policy Governance make governance simpler. But they do not make it easier. Any board that embarks on this path should plan ways to keep itself on track over the long haul. Here are some ideas for sustaining commitment.

Keep Checking Motivation

The first thing directors need to do when starting Policy Governance is to be absolutely clear about why they are starting it. What are the directors' criteria for good corporate governance? Does Policy Governance meet those criteria? Are there shortcomings in existing practices that Policy Governance resolves? Going to the trouble of using a carefully designed, disciplined governance model is not justified by attractive niceties and arcane rules. It is justified, if at all, by greater legitimacy, greater foresight, or greater efficacy in setting the stage for robust and successful management. Only if directors have the reasons for their new commitment clear in the first place will they be able to revisit that motivation when misgivings arise.

Prepare for the Difference

Forewarned is forearmed; the board needs to consider how life will be different after its policies are in place. The sheer departure from usual practice can damage directors' confidence unless they have prepared themselves mentally for the substantial change in board meetings and practices. Considering the likely differences in advance will also help directors gain a sense of what being on track with Policy Governance looks like and alert them to the symptoms of falling off track.

Reports from senior management will be prepared and read against defined criteria, and board discussions will be largely on existing policy. Consequently, meetings may be shorter or less frequent or both, with occasional longer debates about ends or particularly sensitive means topics. Directors will be likely to spend more time deliberating with each other rather than focusing on senior management's proposals. There will be far more talk about owners' interests and far less about the management of operations. There will be less fragmentation and more speaking with one voice. Board policies will be the central focus of every meeting either because they are being reviewed or because they are being monitored. Monitoring performance will be more routine and more focused, so it will not take up significant meeting time except when there is underperformance.

Honor the Chair's Role

The importance of the chair's role as chief governance officer—as distinct from any executive role—in keeping the board to its governance commitment was discussed in Chapter Three and is further addressed in Appendixes B and C. Here we simply reiterate that the chair's role is to keep the board to its word, as the board itself has set out in Governance Process and Board-Management Delegation policies. At the same time, if group responsibility is to be meaningful, the role of the chair as protector of the board's discipline and integrity of process cannot be taken by other directors as relieving them of responsibility for those things. Of course the other directors have not been given the power of the gavel, but they are culpable if they sit silently through failures of board discipline. In addition to being held accountable for the performance of his or her role, the chair deserves to be able to rely on directors for support in maintaining governance integrity.

Establish CEO Support

CEOs can be enormously supportive in helping boards stay on course. Every time CEOs submit a monitoring report or raise a question linked to a particular board policy, they are reinforcing the importance not only of that policy but of the policy system. Every time they explain to a board how they have reasonably interpreted a particular board policy, they are increasing the board's understanding not only of the policy but of the power of the board's words. Every time CEOs relate some board discussion to the relevant policy, they sustain the policy as a living document, even when they are focusing on why the policy needs to be changed. In any event, the integrity and utility of policies is continually improved.

Invest in Director Recruitment, Orientation, and Education

Directors should be recruited for their interest and competence in the owner-driven, long-range big picture, not for their skill or experience in advising on operations. Their relevant business acumen arises from judgment and expertise that enables them to understand the company's economic environment, markets, risk, and other such macro-concerns. Although directors need to be wise generalists, it is not important that they have the skill to run the company they govern. Owners need a board that governs, not one that acts as a management consultancy. Governance policy work requires that directors be willing and able to explore the values behind issues rather than taking and even solving issues at face value. In addition, directors must be assertive and persuasive yet able to value and be respectful of group process, diversity, and the board's final vote.

Thorough director orientation to the board and its highly designed governance process is as vital as orientation to the company itself. Even without Policy Governance, the work of the board is different from the work of management and deserves specialized attention. Policy Governance, as an unfamiliar paradigm, is especially different, intensifying the need for orientation. Governance experience acquired on traditional boards provides a comparative reference and top-level experience, but helps little—and may even interfere—with understanding a new approach. Companies typically invest a lot in the ongoing training of managers. There is no justification for treating the continuing education of directors as any less important, particularly as governance becomes a more precise endeavor.

Set Appropriate Director Compensation

Sustaining board commitment has to involve consideration of director compensation. The Policy Governance framework makes no direct statement about directors' compensation. More important, it has no implications that would oppose determining directors' compensation by the market. Having said that, we can affirm that all other things being equal, governance will proceed more effectively with a small board of adequately paid directors than with a larger group of inadequately paid directors.

Further, setting part of ordinary compensation on a meeting-by-meeting basis seems more akin to paying for piecework in a factory or paying a consultant than to paying someone for an overall accountability (as is done, for example, for upper management).

Meeting supplements may also have the distressing potential to act as an incentive for more meetings than necessary (though the busy directors we know would find that idea amusing). We support reducing or eliminating meeting-by-meeting supplements, even if that change needs to be balanced by raising the overall director compensation that is tied simply to fulfilling a highly responsible job.

In any event, a good board is the cost of adequate shareholder control. The CEO is not in a position to set his or her boss's pay scale, so the decisions on the compensation, perquisites, and logistical costs appropriate to governance for a given company are board decisions, not management decisions.

Screen Other Governance Wisdom

Increasing interest in corporate governance over the past couple of decades has led to a wealth of advice and information for boards. Most of the counsel is from wise and experienced authors and consultants but is based on governance as it is known today. With the introduction of a new governance model, some amount of that wisdom loses relevance and some becomes outmoded. It is no denigration of football wisdom to say that when a football player switches to playing baseball, much of that wisdom loses its utility. This is the price of a paradigm shift. The Policy Governance board needs to evaluate all governance advice carefully to ensure that it will help rather than damage the board's ability to maintain model consistency, that is, to govern with a coherent, single set of rules. Even brilliant new methods are not really improvements unless they contribute to an improved *system*.

Holding Effective Board Meetings

The greatest single discipline for the board to learn is the discipline of dealing with every issue through policy. The importance of this point cannot be overemphasized. In fact, once this point is grasped, any board may be on its way to finding a more value-based, high-leverage way to fulfill its accountability to owners.

Three Questions for Staying on Track

Before dealing with *any* issue that comes to the board table, the board should ask itself three questions:

1. What is the policy category for this issue?
2. What have we already said in our policy about this issue?
3. Are we happy with what we have already said, or do we wish to change it?

It is worth repeating that the design of Policy Governance is such that *whatever* issue comes up, the board will already have said something that covers it, due to the nested bowl assembly of board decisions in the policy system. The directors may decide that whatever has been said is insufficiently detailed, but always *something* will have been said.

Always asking these three questions is what ensures that the board's policy manual does not sit on the corporate secretary's shelf, but is complete, current, and in constant use by the CEO and by every director during every meeting and for every issue. *The policies remain complete and current because no board decision is ever made without reference to them.*

Agendas

Because the board needs to govern itself first, the board's agendas must be set by the board for the board. Board meetings in the Policy Governance framework are not management's meetings for the board. The logistics and mechanics of meetings can certainly be assigned to the CEO (as they are in the "Communication to and Support of the Board" policy, shown in Exhibit 5.5), but content and process belong to the board itself. This does not mean that the

CEO is shut out of the board's deliberations in any way. It just means that the CEO is not responsible for them.

Describing the board's job in terms of the values the board adds (and not the activities it engages in) creates what is in effect a *perpetual agenda*—a statement of what the board will always be working on. (Policy 1.4 in Appendix E is an example of such a job description.) From this description of the ongoing board job, the board derives the annual calendar and the individual meetings needed to produce the board's values-added. This process creates board-determined agendas that become tools in themselves for keeping the board in the right direction. Happily, it is not necessary that the full board go too far into the specifics of this meeting-by-meeting agenda planning. As the board goes into more detail (progressing, in our analogy, toward smaller bowls), it can safely stop where it wishes because the chair will take over where the full board stops.

Some corporate boards must please a regulatory or legal requirement that the board decide on something that by rights should be decided by management within the board's higher level of policy. In these cases, a consent agenda may be used to signal board assent without causing what would amount to *un*delegation against the board's better judgment. These are occasions in which the board is obligated to owners to govern well and ethically *despite* law and regulations, and yet of course the law must still be obeyed.

Voting

The principle that the board speaks with one voice does not mean that everyone on the board has to vote the same way. It simply means that once the board has spoken (as determined by the applicable voting rules), everyone needs to honor the decision as a proper board decision. Corporate boards sometimes set such a premium on unanimity that a single vote against, say, a merger (to reiterate a point made previously) can throw analysts and shareholders into fits of reaction. Yet to insist on unanimity represents a major threat to the board's ability to encourage diversity at the board table.

If boards are to be honest deliberators of corporate destiny, dissent on the board cannot be viewed as a disturbing occurrence signifying lack of commitment to the majority decision. Instead, free voting that is always followed by total dedication to the winning vote needs to become the norm, and this norm should be established long before a highly visible and sensitive vote (like a merger decision) is on the table. Board decision making should be a deliberation among honest differences of opinion, not a public relations tool.

Conducting Board Self-Evaluation

Self-evaluation is a powerful tool to help directors maintain their intended discipline. Policy Governance turns such evaluation into a straightforward process, for the board will have described governance excellence in its Governance Process and Board-Management Delegation policies. This method of evaluation is greatly to be recommended over off-the-shelf evaluation forms, which assess the board on criteria it may never have accepted. With the criteria already in place, all that remains to be decided is the method and frequency with which the board will check on itself.

Board evaluation generally takes the form of self-evaluation, although there is nothing to prevent a board from inviting owners (where practical) or management to participate in rating the board against those policies on which these observers are competent to comment. We suggest that the board take at least a few minutes at the end of each meeting to evaluate itself against one or more of its policies. The board might also wish to undertake an annual review of its performance against all its Governance Process and Board-Management Delegation policies. In our experience, however, it is the meeting-by-meeting comparison to the basic template of board behavior that seems the best guarantee of excellence. Frequent informal evaluation has a greater effect on actual behavior than infrequent formal evaluations.

Evaluation of individual directors is a touchier process than board self-evaluation. Clearly, what is expected of a director must be derived from what a board needs from its members. Therefore we support the evaluation of individual directors, but only when full board self-evaluation has been underway for some time. In fact, the process of full board self-evaluation not only makes clear what the board needs from its members but also engages directors in the topic of governance excellence. This discussion often goes far toward having the desired effect on individual director behavior, even without formal evaluation.

Behaving Appropriately in Dangerous Moments

It is an unusual company that never faces a crisis—an unexpected cash crunch, the sudden loss of a CEO, a large legal suit, or a shareholder uprising. Tough times can be a big cause of boards' falling off track. When a crisis strikes, the human response is to dive into the murky waters with a lifeline and effect a heroic rescue. For a board operating under Policy Governance, that response is not a wise one. The board must stay on dry land if it is to help the company. Something has to hold firmly to the other end of the lifeline, and that something is the board. The lifeline in Policy Governance is the board's carefully constructed policy system along with the directors' wisdom embedded in the policy content.

A crisis may cause the board to review its policies, but it should never cause the board to set its policy system aside. It is also encouraging to consider that full use of the policy and monitoring system makes many crises less likely to begin with or at least less likely to arrive as surprises.

Making Transitions

Certain company transitions have significant governance implications. The decision to go public is clearly one that belongs to the board as current shareholder representative. Existing shareholder relationships are going to be much diluted, and the board will become accountable to a much wider group of people whose motivations and perspectives may be quite different from those of the current owners.

Mergers, meaning the blending of two or more corporate identities into one, also dilute or in some other way change the relationship between shareholders and the merging company. Because the board is the shareholder representative, Policy Governance would consign the decision on mergers to the board rather than to management.

Acquisitions are a different matter. If the company is agreeing to be acquired, then the same argument regarding the impact on shareholder relations consigns the matter to the board. Remember that the whole issue of shareholder relations—at least the substantive rather than mechanical or clerical aspects of them—is a matter of governance rather than of management. If, in contrast, the company is doing the acquiring, the matter can be treated as any other purchase of an asset. That is, the board may use its Management Limitations policies to put off limits acquisitions of certain types, of certain size, or of certain risk. Within those limits, decisions to acquire other companies are left to the CEO.

There is a whole raft of other matters that have a direct impact on the company's relationship with its owners. Declarations of dividends or stock splits, installation of poison pill provisions, and any other actions that directly affect the typology, degree, or status of owners all rightly fall under the direct purview of the board as owner representative.

Falling Down and Getting Up Again

For a part-time group, being accountable for everything about a company is never going to be an easy challenge. The Policy Governance model makes this challenge manageable but introduces its own challenges. No board is perfect, and it is almost inevitable that there will be stumbles. The model represents an ideal worth striving for, not an easily obtainable and permanent state.

It is useful for a board to anticipate possible scenarios and to discuss the board's proper course should these predicaments or opportunities occur. If the board can anticipate the things likely to tempt it off course and consider how it will handle breakdowns, it will be far better equipped to stick rigorously to its new role and discipline when changes of any kind actually occur.

In our experience, the things that make the most difference for Policy Governance boards in maintaining their gains are the disciplines of asking the three questions suggested earlier and conducting regular board evaluations. Important additional aids are staying in touch with the board's original motivation and having a chair who is assertive about keeping the board to its policy word.

Looking Back, Moving Forward

In this chapter we considered how the board can maintain the discipline required to use the Policy Governance model. However, for many boards the daunting challenge they face right now—given the entrenchment of traditional practices—is how to get underway in the first place. In the next chapter, we complete our explanation of Policy Governance by looking at how a board might get there from where it is today.

Chapter Eight

Getting There from Here

There is no more delicate matter to take in hand,
nor more dangerous to conduct, nor more doubtful
in its success, than to set up as the leader in the
introduction of changes.

—*Niccolò Machiavelli*[1]

In This Chapter

- Starting from where you are now
- Getting through the adoption process
- When full adoption isn't an option
- Applying the model by type of board

Previous chapters have described the Policy Governance model and the board discipline necessary for its use. Here we address implementation practicalities for readers who, convinced themselves that the model offers a credible approach to board leadership, want their board colleagues to consider putting it into action.

Starting Where You Are

Whether or not to adopt the Policy Governance model must be the decision of the whole board, not of one person. The process usually starts, however, with one person who is convinced that the model represents a useful advance and who is willing to champion early stages of the adoption process.

The model's simplicity might make adoption look straightforward, but leaving many of the comforts of conventional wisdom behind is never easy. Boards are permanent bodies that have a longer life than the elected or appointed terms of the individuals within them. As such, they tend to rely on tradition to provide their connective tissue. Additionally, although directors are disciplined individuals, Policy Governance requires group discipline and precision—not something that comes easily to any of us. So we cannot pretend that the transition from old to new will be as effortless as our following commentary might imply. We can only applaud and endorse the courage of any board that ventures boldly on unfamiliar ground in order to improve its ability to create value for owners.

Undertaking a Staged Adoption Process

The Policy Governance adoption process always proceeds in stages, though the pace of those stages varies from board to board. The following sections describe the sequence of stages a board might expect to go through. They correspond roughly to *learning*, *doing*, *testing*, and *adopting*.

Board Education

A board usually becomes aware of Policy Governance after one director or the CEO reads a book or article or hears talk among peers about it and then convinces other directors to examine the model for themselves. Directors might agree to read and discuss this book, for example. They might retain a properly qualified consultant[2] to present an introductory seminar—by far the most effective route. Or they might charge a committee to gather any further information the board wishes. There are several other books on the subject[3]—albeit written for nonprofit and governmental boards—one of which gives detailed descriptions of implementation experiences.[4]

This exploration, or education, stage should not be short-changed, for it lays the foundations of director commitment and understanding needed for the next stages of the journey. Although the decision to adopt or not will be the board's decision alone, senior management should definitely be included in the learning about Policy Governance. Directors will want to know how the model is viewed by the CEO and senior management and to have their understanding and support should the board decide to proceed.

In the initial education stage, besides learning the concepts and implications of the model, directors should identify specific governance goals they hope to accomplish by using the model, such as role clarity, effective use of directors' time, less vulnerability to "where was the board?" charges, or a closer relationship with owners. These goals become the board's criteria for judging the merits of Policy Governance in comparison to other governance practices. We stated in the previous chapter that the board should stay in touch with the reasons for its original commitment; this explicit list of goals will eventually help directors do that. At this first stage, however, the board's commitment to Policy Governance is only to take the next step, not to make a final commitment. Because of the enormity of the changes that come with adoption, we recommend taking one step at a time; only in the very last step does the board make its formal decision to move completely into the Policy Governance framework. The final step, in any case, cannot be taken until the board has prepared its policies in the new format and those policies are ready for use.

Policy Drafting

The next step then is to draft a complete set of board policies. This involves a substantial amount of time and effort—a minimum of two full days, assuming expert facilitation. Although this may seem like a lot of time, it is a capital investment in the board's capability to govern. Given the importance of the governing job to the future of the company and the fact that the effort will pay dividends perpetually, the time spent is likely to be seen by directors as among their most productive and enlightening sessions together. Still, the endeavor is a big enough commitment that directors will want to feel reasonably certain the effort is going to be worthwhile.

The policy-drafting process cements an understanding of the model that was previously just an abstraction. It shows directors what the model looks like when tailored to their particular company. Although the policy drafting is interesting and enriching, it is painstaking as well, partly because it requires great care in using words precisely and partly because it demands maintaining consistency with an as yet unfamiliar framework and architecture.

Directors may wish to get qualified consulting assistance or proceed on their own. The former choice costs more at the outset but is probably the more economical in the long run. For the latter route, policy samples in Appendix E can serve as templates. We warn, however, against trying to adapt preexisting corporate documents. In fact, we have never seen that approach taken successfully, for a company's traditional documents do not observe the distinctions that make the model work—the differentiation of ends and means, the boundary-setting control of management's means, the cascading treatment of sizes of decisions, and the totality of board decisions captured in a centralized, succinct master document.

For some policies—usually ones concerning risk, dealing in company shares, and the company's financial condition—extra study of the options and of the implications of various provisions must take place outside the initial drafting session and be brought back to the board. Further, the board may wish to give the CEO (who has been consulted, of course, during the drafting) additional time to comment on the feasibility of the expectations being considered in one or more of the Ends policies and Management Limitations policies. Although the CEO does not have the final say, it would obviously be foolish for the board to move ahead without fully considering the CEO's insights. But whatever the delay, it is more important to be accurate and complete in these emerging policies than to be fast, with one exception.

Despite the deliberateness with which the board must check on the adequacy of its policy drafts, it is better for the board to do the *initial* drafting rapidly and in a single session and to avoid introducing legal and other complicating factors during that creative period. That momentum and a sense of at least temporary completion are essential if directors are to accomplish such an impressive amount of initial work without becoming mired in arcane factors and technicalities, even important technicalities.

However the policies get drafted, it is critical for the board to be certain of two requirements: first, all policies must be written to suit the board's own values, so that the board feels comfortable adopting every word as its own. Remember that *board values* are not a laundry list of all the values held by the individual directors, but values that, taken one at a time, are supported by a majority of directors. Second, even though the board's values control policy content, the model prescriptions must control the framework and architecture through which the values are expressed.

Administrative and Legal Checking

After the board has drafted these policies, we recommend they be examined by legal counsel and whoever else can authoritatively ensure that there are no important legal, financial, or administrative inconsistencies. For instance, the board may have said something in the new documents that is at odds with its bylaws. If so, the board is obliged to act in accordance with bylaws, changing or forgoing the affected policy until and unless the bylaws can be amended to accommodate the new approach.

A word of warning about legal counsel, auditors, and other experts who do not have a thorough understanding of Policy Governance: they may object to particularities simply because they find them strange rather than because they have substantive legal, financial, or administrative concerns. It is important that the board does not allow itself to be diverted by such objections during this testing stage and, within reason, that it educate its advisers on the new governance methodology.

Making the Changeover

Once the board has made all necessary revisions, the outcome should be a draft of a policy manual that covers the board's values and expectations exhaustively and, amazingly, briefly as well. The board is now in a position to safely enact all the policy drafts. The new policies replace almost all preexisting board documents (the board's incorporation document, bylaws, and perhaps certain legally required documents are exceptions—and even the latter can often be incorporated into the policy framework). The official policy manual that emerges upon formal adoption needs to be in a loose-leaf form for easy updating. For the paradox is that despite its supreme position in the conduct of board and executive affairs, the policy collection remains always a working document, open for amendment by the board at any meeting.

The total swap of one system for another is necessary in the adoption stage, lest the board end up trying to operate from two approaches simultaneously—a practice guaranteed to cause both old and new to fail. Therefore we advise against "phasing in," for the same reason that a country changing its rules of the road from driving on the right to driving on the left would be wise not to do so in stages.

Because board meetings after the changeover are going to differ from previous practice, preparation for them needs to be thought about well in advance. As discussed in Chapter Seven, agendas will not look as they did before, but just what they are to look like will take some practice and, in any event, will differ from board to board.

When Full Adoption Isn't an Option

Complete systems are best approached on an all-or-nothing basis, which is simply to say complete systems are best used completely. Policy Governance is a complete system, and, like a watch, if any of its parts are missing the system not only doesn't work but is no longer a system. Partial adoption, then, is a logical inconsistency. However, there may be times when external circumstances or internal doubts delay or prevent a board's adoption of the full model, yet a number of the directors would still like to "move in the direction" of Policy Governance principles.

Moving in a good direction has to be better than not moving at all, so it would be churlish of us not to offer some words of advice. Although we decline to speak of partial adoption of Policy Governance, we can speak of orienting the board toward Policy Governance. The board may still never actually adopt Policy Governance, but at least it will be working in a healthy direction; if it later decides to go further, doing so will not be as much of a leap. When boards find that merely orienting toward Policy Governance is their only option, we recommend that they consider doing at least these things:

- Create a definition of the owner value for which the CEO will be held accountable, and list the major business risks to be avoided.
- Make a clear distinction between board decisions and individual director advice (the former being mandatory and the latter optional from management's perspective).
- Have the chief governance and chief executive roles separately defined and held separately accountable to the board, even if the roles are performed by one person, under whatever title.
- Conduct regular board evaluations.
- Routinely investigate and discuss the board's process of governance and options for its improvement.

Although these adjustments will provide a fraction of the value of the Policy Governance model itself, they will at least augment the clarity and accountability the board brings to its job.

Applying the Model by Type of Board

The Policy Governance model is rooted in the source and nature of governance authority and is, as we asserted in Chapter One, applicable to all types of boards. This does not mean, however, that all boards and organizational types are alike or that they apply the model with identical emphases. Here we look briefly at the use of Policy Governance in three different types of company.

Start-Ups

In many start-ups the board is composed entirely or almost entirely of inside directors. Governance and management are carried out by the same people. The model encourages these persons to separate their governance considerations and actions from their executive considerations and actions, because the roles of board and executive team are not the same. If the habit of separation is begun early, later development (such as the addition of a venture capitalist or other outsider) will already be set on a sensible trajectory. Separation of the board in whole or in part from management may occur in nearly imperceptible stages, hence the need to adopt practices that befit the future before the future arrives.

Joint Ventures

Joint ventures may be the most amenable to changes in governance.[5] Parent companies have a vested interest in a strong board to represent them well, but they also know that a robust CEO is necessary for company success. Weakness in either role can damage the venture partners' investment. The Policy Governance model was built around making both roles strong, in contrast to the seesaw tendencies of traditional governance practices.

Holding Companies

What the parent company requires of subsidiaries can best be phrased in terms of prescribed ends (the shareholder value to accrue to the parent-owner) and minimal proscribed means (allowing a wide range of safe innovation and initiative). Thus the decision authority granted from the holding company to subsidiaries can easily be structured using the decisions-within-decisions architecture accompanied by the any reasonable interpretation rule.[6] If subsidiary boards are to play an optimal role of corporate oversight, holding companies must avoid undermining these boards by giving instructions directly to subsidiary management.

Moving from Governance-Past to Governance-Future

The great promise inherent in the governance model presented in this book is that boards will gain the ability to more powerfully use human talents and wisdom to more certainly fulfill the accountability owed by every company to its owners. Corporate governance has come a long way since the groundbreaking work of Berle and Means,[7] and it is experiencing a truly remarkable renaissance as we move into the twenty-first century, due to increasing fascination with corporate leadership and the growing importance of institutional investors. Governance has become a topic in its own right rather than a pale and subordinate reflection of management.

This book argues that boards of directors should create a type of value not widely or consistently created in today's boardrooms. It champions a powerful, active board that makes decisions of its own and exercises its judgment independent of management (though not in the absence of management). Such a board acts proactively, rather than simply reactively granting blessings to management desires, yet it respects and values management and powerfully authorizes management to do what management does best.

A new order of things always evokes doubts and concerns about its application in the "real world." The thing for directors to remember is that they have the greatest power over the company and that whatever they decide the integrity of governance demands can become reality. Corporate governance reform must, at the end of the day, come from governors, not from executives, consultants, or authors.

We call upon boards to be as innovative, as bold, as flexible, and as logically organized as they expect the modern technologies that serve them to be, whether those technologies concern management, engineering, or information processing. Significant governance system change requires a great deal of rigor, confidence, and courage. Rigor is needed because the board must resist the temptation to adapt the new system to resemble the old. Confidence is needed because the board cannot effect any change unless it is thoroughly convinced of the merits of that change. Courage is needed because once directors are confident that a new approach to their unique challenge best serves owners, they have no responsible choice but to forge ahead boldly and deliberately; they cannot hold back until the new path is made safe and familiar by others.

We submit this book to the corporate world, trusting that its owners, directors, and managers will seize the opportunity for a major breakthrough in corporate leadership. We submit a bold technology of governance based in precepts of accountability, servant-leadership, and group responsibility. We propose a governance operating system that better equips boards to translate the wishes of owners into company performance: causing boards truly to create value.

Appendix A

Glossary

The terms in this glossary are also defined in the text; we have gathered them here for convenient reference. A new paradigm introduces new concepts. Those concepts must be represented by words, sometimes words already in use, sometimes ones created for the occasion. To use familiar words for new concepts reduces the alien impression of the new but risks contaminating the new concept with meanings carried over from the old. Thus in some cases we have decided upon new words and in others used more familiar ones, according to our perceptions of the users' needs.

Any reasonable interpretation rule The authorization to take superiors at their word, to respond to instructions using whatever interpretation the subordinate chooses, so long as he or she can demonstrate that the interpretation is a reasonable one. The any reasonable interpretation rule is indispensable to optimal delegation.

Board-Management Delegation The category of board policy in which the board states the nature and mechanics of the relationship between governance and management.

Chief executive officer (CEO) The initial position with executive authority beneath the governing authority of the full board. The CEO, at the behest of the board, runs the company.

Chief governance officer (CGO) The position of "first among equals" on the board, with the responsibility of ensuring the board follows its own rules and the rules imposed by external authorities.

The job includes but is not limited to chairing meetings. The CGO, at the behest of the board, runs (but is not boss of) the board.

Ends The category of board policy that sets forth the fundamental reason for the company's existence (what the company is *for*), usually thought of as monetary *shareholder value* unless public policy or owners dictate otherwise. Owners are more likely to dictate otherwise in a family or a start-up company, where their interest may extend to more than monetary return. *Ends* is not another word for *results* or *goals*. Further, not all intentions of the company are ends.

Goals and objectives Things to be accomplished. These terms are of great utility in management, but they are problematic in governance in that they do not respect the differentiation between ends and means and often do not respect the principle that decisions come in sizes.

Governance The job of the governing board. Others—but not this text—sometimes use this term to include the entire top leadership.

Governance Process The category of board policy in which the board deals with most of its own means, including the board's relationship with shareholders, its own process, its internal workings (committees, officers), and the discipline to which it is committed.

Management Limitations The category of board policy in which the board proscribes the CEO's means, establishing a free territory of executive decision making within board-set boundaries. By defining what is unacceptable, Management Limitations policies avoid telling management how to manage, thereby keeping the board out of micromanaging or meddling.

Means All issues that aren't ends. All board decisions that do not address ends address means. Means decisions concern methods, conduct, ways of doing business, activities, programs, markets, products, and the like. Virtually all decisions made in a company and by its board are means decisions. Governance itself is a means issue, one that belongs to the board. However, most means issues fall naturally into management.

Owner value What the company owners want the company to be for. Usually owner value is the same as *shareholder value*, except where the law or the nature of the specific company dictates a broader ownership base.

Planning Making decisions today about the future. Because both governance and management can engage in planning, and because planning can apply to both ends and means, the activity, though an important one, does not help in distinguishing the board's job from management's.

Policy A value or perspective that underlies action. Policy Governance policies fall into four categories: Ends, Governance Process, Board-Management Delegation, and Management Limitations. These four categories cover all possible board decisions.

Policy categories The topics by which board policies are grouped. The four Policy Governance policy categories serve governance, not management utility.

Policy levels Degrees of openness to interpretation that are designed into policies. Levels run sequentially from the broadest (least detailed and open to most interpretation) to the narrowest (most detailed and open to the least interpretation). Board policies in each category begin at the broadest level and extend into more detailed levels until they reach a point at which the board can accept any reasonable interpretation of its words. At that point it is safe for the board to stop going into further detail.

Policy Governance® John Carver's conceptual model for leadership by boards of directors—a universal paradigm composed of certain logically derived principles and concepts. The term is a registered service mark of John Carver.

Shareholder value The benefit that is to accrue or has accrued to shareholders from the company or from the equity market and the company. Although public companies invariably define shareholder value in financial terms, the board of a family or other closely held company might choose to include nonfinancial values in the definition. These financial and, if included, nonfinancial values are equivalent to the corporation's ends.

Strategic planning A management tool to ensure the company fulfills the board's Ends policies without violating the board's Management Limitations policies over some multiyear period. Although driven by board expectations, the plan itself is a management document.

Appendix B

The Case for a CGO

In much of the corporate world, the term CEO (*chief executive officer*) is used to designate the top management role. Almost as familiar are the terms COO (*chief operating officer*), CFO (*chief financial officer*), and even CIO (*chief information officer*). A good case can be made for also adopting the term CGO (*chief governance officer*).

One reason for using this new term is merely the cosmetic argument: it fits nicely with the other terms in widespread use. Another benefit is that CGO avoids the verbal struggle between *chair, chairman, chairwoman,* and *chairperson.* However, we have more substantive reasons for our proposition.

Chairman Is an Ambiguous Title

The title of chairman (and its less gender-specific equivalents) has so frequently incorporated an executive component that it does not distinguish governance leadership absolutely from management leadership. This is especially true when one person plays both roles, but even when separate persons wear the titles of chair and CEO, it is not uncommon for the chair to exercise CEO authority anyway.[1]

Such ambiguity in what the title stands for is no problem when it reflects a tolerated overlap between the functions of governance and management. But maintaining a distinction between governance and management is essential in the Policy Governance model, so an ambiguous title for this board role is inappropriate. Using CGO focuses everyone's view of the job on a specific role, one not confounded with any other role.

The Chair's for More Than Chairing

In Policy Governance the job of chairing board meetings is merely one part of the chair's larger responsibility to see that the board gets its job done. This "first among equals" must interpret and carry into fruition those policies created by the board that govern its own job. Some of those policies, as we discussed earlier, relate to the discipline to which the board has committed itself, some to the mechanics of the board-CEO connection, some to more philosophical matters.

When the CGO part of a traditional chair's job is isolated, as it is in Policy Governance, it can be seen to consist primarily of making decisions about governance (not management), always of course within a reasonable interpretation of what the board itself has said in its policies on **Governance Process and Board-Management Delegation.** That role engages the chair in fleshing out many decisions about the way the board will operate, how its committees will function, its manner of self-evaluation, the mechanism of shareholder input, the mechanics of CEO reporting, and whatever else the breadth of board policies in these areas has left to be decided. In short, the chair in Policy Governance is a guarantor of governance integrity, and the term CGO speaks to the fact that the chair has these important and time-consuming demands in addition to the lesser responsibility of chairing meetings.

Given this view of the job, it follows that CGOs ideally will be chosen for their ability to be servant-leaders in the governance environment and for their capacity to attend rigorously to the job of interpreting and fulfilling the requirements of governance that the board has adopted. They might or might not be good with the gavel. Gavel competence is a subsidiary CGO skill, not the central one. A CGO might even choose to appoint someone else to chair single meetings or might rotate the gavel among directors. As Sir Adrian Cadbury has pointed out, "from a statutory point of view there is no need for a company to have a continuing chairman . . . the law looks on the post of chairman as one which is exercised meeting by meeting."[2] Of course, because the CGO is accountable to the board for all aspects of proper governance (that is, for ensuring that governance proceeds in a way consistent with board policies), the CGO remains accountable for an appointee's performance as meeting chair.

It Takes More Than a Title to Clarify a Position

Of course, as anyone who has ever been given a fancier title instead of a raise can attest, titles do not necessarily clarify roles. *President*, for example, does not necessarily denote CEO. That is why, when it does denote the CEO function, companies commonly add "and CEO" to it. Similarly, the title *chair* is not self-explanatory; it might imply "and CEO" whether that addendum is present or not.

Using the term CGO as the title for the position we have been describing here will help clarify that role, at least for as long as company usage can avoid confounding the role of CGO with the role of CEO (as has happened to the chair role and is now reflected in chair as a title). Thus we believe that adopting the term CGO will be of notable usefulness for any board working on governance development. Nevertheless, what is most important is achieving role clarity, whatever the title used.

Conclusion

No one doubts that the words we all use, though objects of our creation, have the power both to channel and facilitate our thoughts and to impede and block them. To paraphrase Churchill, first, we create our words; then they create us. First, we assign words to our concepts; then our words restrict and, perhaps unnecessarily, narrow our concepts. The term *chair* is one that now takes our thoughts in directions that often lead away from proper governance.

Proper governing boards need a point-person for their discipline, a servant-leader for their commitment. Advanced governance requires a specialized role neither, as the chair's role may be, confounded with management nor reduced to only one of the office's functions. *Chief governance officer* is a term with the potential to focus the office holder and the board on fulfilling their proper governance functions.

Chair and CEO

One Person or Two?

The Policy Governance model absolutely requires that the *roles* of *chief governance officer* (called the *chair* in today's boards, see Appendix B) and *chief executive officer* be separated. The power of the model requires that everyone understands which of the roles is being spoken from at every moment. Therefore we argue that an important part of avoiding role confusion is assigning these roles to two different people.

Others also recognize the importance of this step. Mills maintains that "the chairman is the chairman of the board. He is not chairman of the company."[1] Leighton and Thain say the CGO role "requires independent leadership, commitment, focus, time, and talent," and that "it is fundamentally important that [these roles] be separated and not confused."[2] Cadbury notes the difficulty of playing both roles well.[3] Carlsson questions how the board's "independence and ability to carry out its governance role [can] be guaranteed if the chairman, the head of the board, is supposed to govern himself as CEO?"[4] Lorsch and MacIver charge that the "power reversal between the CEO and the board" is "rife with ambiguity and complexity" and that there is a "major need to diminish the CEO's power as leader of the board."[5] Dayton, long-time chairman of Dayton-Hudson, opines, "All my experience and study have convinced me that the chairman of the board should not be the CEO. . . . A chairman/CEO wears two hats at the same time and you just can't do that and look good in both roles."[6] The formidable list of those who argue for separation also includes Knowlton and Millstein,[7] Whitehead,[8] Gogel,[9] Williams,[10] and Patton and Baker.[11]

A growing number of national governance codes also argue—albeit often weakly—for separating these very different offices. A recent survey of three hundred CEOs showed that two-thirds thought the positions should be separated.[12] A McKinsey Investor Opinion Survey[13] found that investors see separation of the positions to be a key factor in board performance, ranking it as important as having a majority of outside directors.

However, in spite of this strong body of opinion, the practice of combining the roles in one person continues to be common practice in several parts of the world. For example, among large U.S. firms, more than 90 percent use the combined position, according to a 1999 Korn-Ferry survey.[14] France *requires* that companies with a single-tier board combine the roles in one person—the Président Directeur Générale.[15] Indeed, it has been pointed out that combining the senior management and board leadership roles in one person is so commonplace that the title *chairman* and its less gender-specific equivalents virtually mean "top executive" to many ears.[16]

We find that the published reasons for combining the CGO and CEO roles in one person can be grouped into six (not precisely separable) categories.

Arguments for Combining the CGO and CEO Roles in One Person

- *It avoids extra baggage.* Separating the CGO and CEO roles results in extra communication layers and inefficiency as the CEO is forced to engage in internal lobbying, taking time away from more important matters. For example, a separate CEO can spend an inordinate amount of time aligning a separate chairman with the CEO's strategy.[17]

- *It sidesteps clashes of authority.* Inasmuch as "no chairman is wholly non-executive,"[18] separate positions "would dilute the power of the CEO to provide effective leadership of the company."[19] Besides, the chair position has a "*natural* power"[20] that can clash with a separate CEO's power. The 2001 conflict at Ford between CEO Jacques Nasser and chairman Bill Ford Jr. exemplifies such a skirmish.[21] Heidrick and Struggles[22] find that many successful nonexecutive chairmen are nonexecutive in name only, causing the separate CEO to be CEO in name only.

- *It keeps accountability clear.* A separate CGO may "shield [a separate] CEO from being held accountable by the board."[23] In any case, having two separate positions creates confusion and blurs accountability.[24]

- *It prevents external confusion.* In current public perception, "chairmen have become chairmen of their companies and not simply of their boards. The position of chairman has no particular *legal* significance, but it has acquired *public* significance."[25] Moreover, separating the CGO and CEO roles could lead to third parties taking advantage of public disagreement between two public spokespersons.[26] At the very least, "outsiders might begin to wonder who is really in charge."[27]

- *It presents no problems that cannot be easily solved.* Admittedly, a single CGO-CEO position reduces board independence from management, but easily available solutions are outsider committees[28] and the lead director role.

    Committees of outside directors. The board does not need freedom from CEO domination because board members can gather in subgroups (for example, compensation and audit committees) that are neither dominated by insiders nor attended by the CEO.

    A lead director. An outside director can be chosen by other outside directors (or may simply emerge) to be more or less a shadow chair. If the person in the combined role falters, the lead director can step in to save the day. A notable case in recent history was the ouster of Chairman and CEO Robert Stempel at General Motors, a skirmish led by outside director John Smale.[29]

- *It is supported by history, social expectations, and a pragmatic view that organizations would be unlikely to accept separate positions.* Bowen[30] states, for example, "Persuaded as I am of its intrinsic appeal, I am convinced that the notion of a separate chairman on corporate boards is not an idea whose time has come." He believes that a board is "unlikely to do battle with an effective CEO over such an issue," and recognizes that "as long as the concept of a separate chairman is so rarely embraced by the corporate world, it will inevitably have more than a slight hint of the unseemly about it." To be sure, under the rules of the game as now played, CEOs who are not appointed to be CGO as well may perceive that the board is sending them a message of no confidence.

Policy Governance offers effective responses to all these arguments. All the reasons for combining the CEO and CGO roles are based on boards' behaving the way they traditionally have, not on the way they should behave. In fact, we believe that *every single objection to filling the separate positions with separate people evaporates if the board governs in the more responsible manner that we have described.*

How Policy Governance Resolves the Impasse

- *It institutes a proper chain of command.* When the board plays its proper governance role, there are no extra communication layers and inefficiency because the CEO neither reports to the CGO nor needs to convince any single director with his or her strategy. The chain of command is board to CEO, not board to CGO to CEO.

- *It supplies clear delegation of authority.* If directors shoulder their responsibility with group integrity, the CGO can have only as much authority as the board explicitly grants. Therefore there can be no clash of authority unless the board has set the stage for it. The most common error by boards that have ostensibly separated the roles is to allow the CGO to act like a CEO anyway, overruling or instructing the real CEO.

- *It establishes clear accountability.* A separate CGO can "shield a [separate] CEO" from accountability only when the board chooses *not* to exercise its authority by holding the CEO directly to account. Confusion and blurred accountability arise not from separate roles but from poor delegation at the outset.

- *It eliminates ambiguity for everyone, including outsiders.* Although the public currently perceives that board and executive leadership are inseparable because that is what many companies have long been teaching, once boards teach themselves something else, public perception will follow. Public confusion begins not when outsiders "wonder who is really in charge" but when *directors* wonder who is really in charge and then pass on their ambiguity.

- *It preserves the board's wholeness.* Committees are subordinate to the whole board. It defies common sense to maintain that whatever is suspect about the composition of the whole can be cleansed by integrity in its subordinate parts. Policy Governance causes the board to bear *group* responsibility and to understand that *all* directors work for shareholders.

- *It preserves authority of the CGO's role.* The supposed solution of having a lead director who can take over from a faltering CGO who is also a CEO exemplifies the all-too-human tendency to go to great lengths to avoid fixing a real problem—a compromised role that makes it difficult for the CGO to fulfill certain challenges when the chips are down. The CGO role in Policy Governance is not weak or unimportant; the CGO is not reduced to being percussive with a gavel. It is a role central to the board's responsibility to act as an authoritative group. With an adequate CGO who helps the board maintain its Policy Governance discipline, the lead director is not needed. Relying on a lead director is much like attending with great care to one's emergency parachute while putting very little thought into the design of the primary one.

- *It makes change more desirable than going along with tradition.* An effective board would not countenance inertia as a reason for not making necessary changes in management; it should not accept it in governance either. Sociopolitical reasons for maintaining the status quo have *nothing to do with pursuing the integrity of board leadership*.

It is true that current research has failed to show a difference in corporate performance between companies with separated roles and those with combined roles. But as long as separate chairs are so frequently de facto CEOs (thereby rendering the positions separate in name only), the research has not in fact addressed the question.

Combining the CEO and CGO roles in one person is a rational action only as long as corporate governance is an underdeveloped role. Once the board attains group responsibility, it requires undiluted governance leadership, and that is best achieved by a separate chief governance officer.

Appendix D

Inside Directors

Inside (U.S. usage) or *executive* (U.K. usage) directors are present on most company boards worldwide. The characteristics that make a director either *inside* or *outside* are not as clear as the words might convey. The ambiguity fuels active debate among legal scholars, academics, and shareholder activists. Certainly, executives who work directly for the CEO are insiders. But investment bankers and lawyers retained by the CEO may also be so designated, along with the company's former executives. In this discussion, we consider the CEO who sits on the board to be an inside director, as is anyone else on the board whose work life with respect to the company is totally or substantially controlled by the CEO.

In this appendix, we challenge the notion that an organization needs insiders, *any* insiders, on the board. In the text we have argued that a board's job is to speak, authoritatively and disinterestedly, for owners. The board's job is not to be an adviser to management. To fulfill its governance role, the board has no need to fill its seats with members of management. If the board's single task is to be a microcosm of ownership rather than an arm of management, one has to ask what equips insiders to carry out that task with more competence, personal responsibility, or wisdom than outside directors would have. In particular, one has to ask what gives them enough of these qualities to outweigh their obvious conflict of roles.

Indeed, for managers to be part of the body for whom they work presents a conflict of interest so obvious that only the blessing of long tradition imparts to the practice a measure of credibility. When on the board, managers are in a position to serve their own interests over those of shareholders. The fact that most have too much integrity to consciously do that is immaterial when the goal should be to build a system free of easily avoidable conflicts. Further, inasmuch as board agendas and information are largely management-generated in traditional governance, the influence of managers over the board is already significant without their being on the board as well.

There must be a powerful influence keeping such a practice in place. And there is. Underpowered governance cannot adequately play its role in the chain of command between owners and management. To render this inadequacy less obvious, a protocol has emerged to give the appearance that the board is playing a superior role and is in charge. Nonprofit and governmental boards often gain that appearance by meddling in small aspects of management. Corporate directors, however, are usually too sophisticated about management to fall into the micromanaging trap. So one way to have the board apparently stay at arm's length (because its job is not to manage), yet not appear to be a rubber stamp, is to include in board thinking and composition to some degree the same issues and persons as inhabit management. After all, if outside directors aren't sure what their job is, the organization can put enough managers on the board to tell them what it is—without having it appear that the subordinate is bossing the superior.

Only the long-standing, traditionally condoned hegemony of management over the governance process explains this practice. And to the extent that corporate governance exists as a stepchild of management rather than a practice important in its own right, organizations will continue to drag the language, the skills, the reporting formats, and the personalities of management into the boardroom. Organizations have confounded governance and management so thoroughly that it has become impossible for a traditional board to function unless supplied with insiders who "really know what is going on." Organizations have treated governance as merely an extension of management in group form for so long that peppering or even loading the board with insiders seems an undeniably necessary approach.

Once this step has been taken, the practice is to patch over the conflict of interest and inherent contradiction by preparing lists of what inside directors do and what outside directors do. For example, audit committees should be composed of outsiders (though the practice of including insiders on them lingers). These valiant attempts to outline who should do what often reveal that the outsiders get most of the chores one would associate with governance,[1] whereas insiders get to participate in things that are more, well, inside.

We are by no means challenging the need to have the CEO and other managers available to the board. We are not arguing for the CEO—or other executives when appropriate—to be absent from board meetings. We are arguing that it is not necessary to be *on* the board to be very productive *with* the board. In fact, boards would be unwise in the extreme to do their important work without the counsel and information that executives can supply. However, there is *nothing* in proper corporate governance that necessitates the *voting* presence of insiders on the board.

Moreover, many have pointed out, even argued in detail, that the skills needed for management and governance are quite different.[2] Management is, or should be, chosen for its ability to run the company rather than for its ability to interpret shareholders. When a director is chosen, surely the uppermost qualification is the capability to govern. Of course any individual manager might also have governance abilities, and any director might also have the skills or temperament fitted to manage the enterprise. But it is the required skill, not optional ones, that should predominate as a qualification for the job.

The only real argument against removing inside directors from boards is the immediate shock that it will deliver to analysts, investors, and the insiders themselves. But analysts and investors learn new things every day, and we aver they can learn quickly that a lack of insiders does not constitute lack of faith in management. Other than the short-lived tremor of change itself, then, there is simply *no downside* to eliminating insiders from boards of directors, once boards take up the gauntlet to truly govern.

Sample Board Policies
Under Policy Governance

In the Policy Governance model, the principles on which the board bases its authority are expressed in terms of the receiving (from owners) and the giving away (largely to management) of that authority. The documents that express the decisions the board makes about receiving and giving away authority can be called whatever the board chooses but in the model are referred to as *policies*. Although the model provides the principles on which the board's job is based and a framework of policy design that makes it possible for the board to organize and leverage all its decisions so that they cover the entire company, *the model does not dictate the exact content or level of detail of the board's policies*, only the guidelines under which they are created. The policy framework of Policy Governance is just that—a carefully crafted *framework* built to be filled in by individual boards.

Therefore, although the policies displayed as examples in this appendix are consistent with the Policy Governance model, they are not necessarily the policies a given board should have. Even when a particular policy topic is useful for a given board, the policy content may not necessarily be what that board should adopt. Moreover, the depth, or level, of detail shown here may not be what a given board would choose. These policies are samples, and boards should expect to adapt them or to create their own policies as necessary. Unlike the text, the samples use our new term *CGO* instead of *chair*.

These policy samples, or templates, are arranged in the four policy categories described in the text. Each policy is titled with its subject matter and its policy category. Here is a brief recapitulation of the policy categories, in order of their appearance in these pages:

- **Governance Process.** This category deals with all issues of the board's job and the relationship between the board and others (except for the special relationship with the CEO). Policies found in this category describe the board's job, the chief governance officer's job, board committee jobs, and the board's link to shareholders.

- **Board-Management Delegation.** This category describes the way in which the board connects governance and management. Because most boards choose to use a CEO, these policies ordinarily describe the CEO's job, the nature of executive delegation, and the method of monitoring, evaluating, and compensating the CEO.

- **Ends.** This category is the only one that addresses company ends rather than means. In it the board describes the owner value the CEO will operate the company to achieve. Although family corporations and some other companies may have central reasons for existence other than shareholder value seen in monetary terms, large publicly traded companies are quite likely not only to focus on shareholder value alone as the company's ends but to rename this category Shareholder Value. As a result of this straightforward focus, this category is often an extraordinarily brief one. (Sample policies, all at the broadest level, are offered for publicly traded companies and for an individual proprietorship, a start-up company of eager comrades, and a family business.)

- **Management Limitations.** This category prohibits the management methods, conduct, circumstances, practices, and so forth that the board sees as unacceptable means while achieving the defined ends. It is verbally negative but psychologically positive in that the CEO is authorized to make any decisions and engage in any activities that do not violate these policies.

Each policy follows an architecture that reflects the need to make large decisions first, the next smaller ones next, and so forth, as set out in the model. As before, *large* and *small* do not correspond to *important* and *unimportant* but to *broad* and *narrow*. A board can stop at any level, and so boards deciding on their own policies might have policies either briefer than these or more extensive. There are a number of points in these samples that require proper legal review. Nothing that appears in these samples is intended to replace the need for legal advice.

Table of Contents

3.0 Purpose of Our Company [for an entrepreneurial start-up group]

3.0 Center of Family Occupational Life [for a family-owned business]

Policy Category: Management Limitations

4.0 Basic Executive Constraints

    4.1 Treatment of Stakeholders

    4.2 Treatment of Employees

    4.3 Financial Planning and Budgeting

    4.4 Financial Condition and Activities

    4.5 Emergency Loss of CEO

    4.6 Asset Protection

    4.7 Investments

    4.8 Compensation and Benefits

    4.9 Communication to and Support of the Board

    4.10 Trading in Company Securities

    4.11 Diversification

    4.12 Dealings with Shareholders

Policy 1.0: Governance Commitment

Policy Category: Governance Process

The purpose of the board, on behalf of the shareholders, is to see to it that the company (a) achieves appropriate results for shareholders and (b) avoids unacceptable actions and situations.

1. **Accountability Philosophy.** The board's fundamental accountability is to the shareholders.
2. **Social Responsibility.** Although the board accepts as its primary obligation to operate in the best interests of shareholders, that fidelity is tempered by an obligation to the social order and good citizenship.
3. **Governing Style.** The board will govern lawfully with an emphasis on (a) outward vision rather than an internal preoccu-

pation, (b) encouragement of diversity in viewpoints, (c) strategic leadership more than administrative detail, (d) clear distinction of board and chief executive roles, (e) collective rather than individual decisions, (f) the future rather than the past or present, and (g) proactivity rather than reactivity.

4. **Board Job Description.** The specific job outputs (values-added) of the board, as informed agent of the shareholders, are those that ensure an unbroken chain of accountability from shareholders to company performance.

5. **Board-Shareholder Linkage.** As the representative of the shareholders' interests, the board will maintain a credible and continuing link between owners and operators.

6. **Agenda Planning.** To accomplish its job products with a governance style consistent with board policies, the board will follow an annual agenda that (a) completes a reexploration of Ends policies, (b) reexamines Management Limitations policies and the sufficiency of their protection from risk, and (c) continually improves board performance through board education, rich input, and deliberation.

7. **CGO's Role.** The chief governance officer (CGO) ensures the integrity of the board's process and, secondarily, represents the board as needed to outside parties, including but not limited to shareholders.

8. **Directors' Conduct.** The board commits itself and its members to ethical, businesslike, and lawful conduct, including members' proper use of authority and appropriate decorum when acting as directors.

9. **Committee Principles.** Board committees, when used, will be assigned so as to reinforce the wholeness of the board's job and so as never to interfere with delegation from board to CEO.

10. **Committee Structure.** Board committees are those set forth by board action, along with their job products, time lines, and board-authorized use of funds and management time. Unless otherwise stated, a committee ceases to exist as soon as its task is complete.

11. **Cost of Governance.** The board will consciously invest in its ability to govern competently and wisely.

Policy 1.1: Accountability Philosophy

Policy Category: Governance Process

The board's fundamental accountability is to the shareholders.

1. The board is the sole position in the corporation to exercise the owner representative role with respect to shareholders. This role is undelegable.
2. The primary test of board performance is always to be viewed with respect to its fundamental accountability to shareholders.
3. Notwithstanding the primacy of, and without diluting, that accountability, the board recognizes the obligation of any person or company to ethical and conscientious behavior in the society.
4. The board's accountability will be fulfilled through its own actions and through a careful framework of delegation to anyone or any entity to whom the board grants a portion of its authority.
    A. Accountability to shareholders will be discharged primarily through the board's creation of appropriate Ends policies and cautious Management Limitations policies, holding the CEO accountable to the board for fulfillment.
    B. Accountability to law, nonequity stakeholders, and the general society will be discharged primarily through the board's creation of Management Limitations policies cognizant of the board's values concerning lawfulness and ethics.

Policy 1.2: Social Responsibility

Policy Category: Governance Process

Although the board accepts as its primary obligation to operate in the best interests of shareholders, that fidelity is tempered by an obligation to the social order and good citizenship.

1. The company will act lawfully, honoring transparency and declared ethical standards regardless of any negative impact on shareholder value.
2. In determining company Ends from the wide variety of shareholder interests, the board will give greater weight to long-term shareholder value due to the social benefit of stable corporate longevity.
3. Material charitable contributions must be justifiable by expected eventual effect on shareholder value—through advertising effect, employee morale effect, or other good business practice—unless otherwise directed by shareholder input.

Policy 1.3: Governing Style

Policy Category: Governance Process

The board will govern lawfully with an emphasis on (a) outward vision rather than an internal preoccupation, (b) encouragement of diversity in viewpoints, (c) strategic leadership more than administrative detail, (d) clear distinction of board and chief executive roles, (e) collective rather than individual decisions, (f) the future rather than the past or present, and (g) proactivity rather than reactivity.

1. The board will cultivate a sense of group responsibility. The board, not the management, will be responsible for excellence in governing. The board will be the initiator of policy, not merely a reactor to management initiatives. The board may use the expertise of individual members to enhance the ability of the board as a body, while avoiding substituting individual judgments for the board's values.
2. The board will direct, control, and inspire the organization through the careful establishment of broad written policies reflecting the board's values and perspectives. The board's major policy focus will be on shareholder value and the limitation of risk, not on management methods of attaining those effects.

3. The board will enforce upon itself whatever discipline is needed to govern with excellence. Discipline will apply to matters such as attendance, preparation for meetings, policymaking principles, respect of roles, and ensuring the continuance of governance capability. Although the board can change its governance process policies at any time, it will observe them scrupulously while in force.

4. Continual board development will include orientation of new directors in the board's governance process and periodic board discussion of process improvement.

5. The board will not allow the CGO, any director, or any committee of the board to hinder the fulfillment of its commitments or be an excuse for not fulfilling those commitments.

6. The board will monitor and discuss the board's process and performance at each meeting. Self-monitoring will include comparison of board activity and discipline to policies in the Governance Process and Board-Management Delegation categories.

Policy 1.4: Board Job Description

Policy Category: Governance Process

The board's specific job outputs, as informed agent of the shareholders, are those that ensure an unbroken chain of accountability from shareholders to company performance.

1. A credible link between shareholders and the operational company.

2. Written governing policies that address the broadest levels of all company decisions and situations.

    A. *Ends policies:* expected company performance in terms of benefits and recipients of benefits desired by owners.

    B. *Management Limitations policies:* constraints on executive authority that establish the prudence and ethics boundaries within which all executive activity and decisions must take place.

C. *Governance Process policies*: specification of how the board conceives, carries out and monitors, and ensures long-term competence in its own task.

D. *Board-Management Delegation policies*: how power is delegated and its proper use monitored; the CEO's role, authority, and accountability.

3. Successful management performance on expectations stated in policy categories 2A and 2B above.

Policy 1.5: Board-Shareholder Linkage

Policy Category: Governance Process

As the representative of the shareholders' interests, the board will maintain a credible and continuing link between owners and operators.

1. The process of governance will be philosophically aligned with maintaining this link.
   A. As a body, the board will represent all shareholders, not just majority or large block shareholders.
2. The mechanics of relationship will be in the service of maintaining this link.
   A. The board will, as a body or as assigned directors, meet with institutional investors regularly and with other investors as practical.
   B. The board will have shareholders surveyed or otherwise will elicit shareholder desires both in and outside of annual general meetings.
   C. The board will, through Management Limitations policy, require transparency and accuracy in management's shareholder relations.

Policy 1.6: Agenda Planning

Policy Category: Governance Process

To accomplish its job with a governance style consistent with board policies, the board will follow an annual agenda that (a) completes a reexploration of Ends policies, (b) reexamines Management Limitations policies and the sufficiency of their protection from risk, and (c) continually improves board performance through board education, rich input, and deliberation.

1. The cycle will conclude each year on the last day of [*month*] so that administrative planning and budgeting can be based on accomplishing a one-year segment of the board's stated Ends.
2. The cycle will start with the board's development of its agenda for the next year.
3. Throughout the year, the board will attend to consent agenda items as expeditiously as possible.
4. Other than due care confirmation, CEO monitoring will be included on the agenda only when, in majority director opinion, monitoring reports fail to demonstrate policy fulfillment or when policy criteria are to be debated.
5. CEO remuneration will be decided after a review of monitoring reports received in the last year, as soon as practical during the first quarter.
6. The CGO's finalization of each meeting agenda will provide the flexibility to include emerging issues and the recommendation of additional items by individual directors.

Policy 1.7: CGO'S ROLE

Policy Category: Governance Process

The chief governance officer (CGO) ensures the integrity of the board's process and, secondarily, represents the board as needed to outside parties, including but not limited to shareholders.

1. The job result of the CGO is that the board behaves consistently with its own rules and those legitimately imposed on it from outside the organization.
   A. Meeting discussion content will be only those issues that, according to board policy, clearly belong to the board to decide, not to the CEO.

B. Deliberation will be fair, open, and thorough, but also timely, orderly, and kept to the point.

2. The authority of the CGO consists in making decisions that fall within topics covered by board policies on Governance Process and Board-Management Delegation, with the exception of (a) employment or termination of a CEO and (b) any portions of this authority that the board specifically delegates to others. The CGO is authorized to use any reasonable interpretation of the provisions in Governance Process and Board-Management Delegation policies.

   A. The CGO is empowered to chair board meetings with all the commonly accepted power of that position (for example, ruling, recognizing).

   B. The CGO has no authority to make decisions about or within the Ends and Management Limitations policy areas.

   C. The CGO may represent the board to outside parties in announcing board-stated positions and in stating decisions and interpretations in the area delegated to her or him.

   D. The CGO may delegate any part of his or her authority to another director but remains accountable for its use.

Policy 1.8: Directors' Conduct

Policy Category: Governance Process

The board commits itself and its members to ethical, businesslike, and lawful conduct, including members' proper use of authority and appropriate decorum when acting as directors.

1. Members must have loyalty to the shareholders, unconflicted by loyalties to management, other organizations, and any self-interest.

2. Members must avoid conflict of interest with respect to their fiduciary responsibility.

   A. There will be no self-dealing or business by a member with the organization except where approved by the board and appropriately disclosed as required by the [regulatory *authorities*]. Members will annually disclose their involvements with other organizations, with vendors, or with any associations as required by the [*regulatory authorities*], whether or not such involvement might be or might reasonably be seen to be a conflict.

B. When the board is to decide on an issue about which a member has an unavoidable conflict of interest, that member shall absent herself or himself without comment from not only the vote but also the deliberation.

3. Board members may not attempt to exercise individual authority over the organization.

A. Members' interaction with the CEO or with management must recognize the lack of authority vested in individuals except when explicitly board authorized.

B. All external communications will be through the CGO or CEO. Unavoidable member interaction with shareholders, the public, the press, or other entities must recognize the same limitation and the inability of any board member to speak for the board or the corporation.

C. Except for participation in board deliberation about whether reasonable interpretation of board policy has been achieved by the CEO, members will not express individual judgments of performance of employees or of the CEO.

4. Members will respect the confidentiality appropriate to issues of a sensitive nature.

5. Members will be properly prepared for board deliberation.

6. In the trading of the company's securities while in possession of confidential information, the board commits itself and its individual directors to ethical conduct beyond the requirements of law and [*regulatory authority*] regulations, under penalty of removal from the board.

A. There will be no trading or causing of trading while in possession of material nonpublic information.

i. No director may purchase or sell any security of the company, whether or not issued by the company, while in possession of material nonpublic information concerning the security.

ii. No director who knows of material nonpublic information may communicate that information to any other person if he or she has reason to believe that the information may be improperly used in connection with securities trading.

iii. Directors, directors' spouses, other persons living in directors' households, minor children, and entities over which such person exercise control (hereafter called "Covered Persons") must not trade in company securities without prior clearance.

    a. No Covered Person may, indirectly or directly, purchase or sell any security issued by the company without requesting and receiving prior approval from corporate counsel (the "Compliance Officer"), who will examine and safeguard the legality and policy-compliance of the transaction.

    b. Records will be kept of the date each request is received, and the date and time each request is approved or disapproved. Unless revoked, a grant of permission will remain valid until the closing of trading two business days following the day on which it was granted.

    c. Requests will be approved only for trading that is to occur during the three-week period starting on the third business day after a release of quarterly or annual financial results including adequate comment on new developments during the period. When relative stability is lacking in the company's operations and the market for its securities or when material nonpublic information becomes known to the requestor (director), preclearance may be denied during this window period.

    d. Appeal of any decision of the Compliance Officer can be made only to the Audit Committee.

    iv. Covered Persons are prohibited from engaging in certain trading practices without advance approval of the Audit Committee.

        a. Covered Persons who purchase company securities (other than from the company, such as by exercise of stock options) must retain such securities for at least six months.

        b. Covered persons may not sell the company's securities short.

        c. Covered Persons may not buy or sell puts or calls on the company's securities. This prohibition does not restrict the exercise of options granted by the company, but rather prohibits Covered Persons from writing, buying, or selling options in the market, such as listed options.

        d. Covered Persons may not purchase the company's securities on margin, except in connection with very short term borrowing related to the cashless exercise of stock options granted by the company.

B. All directors are required to sign an acknowledgement and certification of this policy.

Policy 1.9: Committee Principles

Policy Category: Governance Process

Board committees, when used, will be assigned so as to reinforce the wholeness of the board's job and so as never to interfere with delegation from board to CEO.

1. Board committees are to help the board do its job, not to help, advise, or exercise authority over management. Committees will assist the board ordinarily by preparing policy alternatives and implications for board deliberation or by performing specific audit functions.

2. Board committees may not speak or act for the board except when formally given such authority for specific and time-limited purposes.
3. Expectations, composition, and authority of each committee will be carefully stated in the "Committee Structure" policy in order to establish performance time lines and the monitoring schedule of committee work, as well as to avoid conflicting with authority delegated to the CEO.
4. Because the CEO works for the full board, he or she will not be required to obtain approval of a board committee before an executive action except where such action is a board action rather than an executive action and such board authority has formally been given the committee and the committee has directed the CEO to carry out said board action (for example, the grant of stock options).
5. Unless otherwise stated in the "Committee Structure" policy, a committee ceases to exist as soon as its task is complete.
6. A committee is a board committee only when its existence and charge come from the board, whether or not directors sit on the committee. This policy does not apply to committees formed under the authority of the CEO.

Policy 1.10: Committee Structure

Policy Category: Governance Process

Board committees are those set forth by board action, along with their job products, time lines, and board-authorized use of funds and management time. Unless otherwise stated, a committee ceases to exist as soon as its task is complete.

1. Audit Committee
    A. *Products:* (a) annual specification of scope of audit prior to outside audit consistent with board monitoring policy; (b) assessment of auditor independence; (c) confirmation of

integrity of audit product following completion of audit; choice of auditor for shareholder consideration.

B. *Authority:* to direct work of outside auditors, to use management time as needed for administrative support, and to direct work of outside counsel hired by the board for matters related to the audit. For all activities including audit, use of no more than [*money amount*].

2. Stock Option Committee

A. *Product:* annual grant and conditions of grant of stock options to employees and consultants for board consideration within the terms specified by the stock option plan under which said grant is made.

B. *Authority:* use of no more than [*amount*] hours of management time and [*money amount*] for outside counsel.

3. Director Development Committee

A. *Products:* (a) properly screened potential board members, by no later than February each year, though no more candidates are required to be presented to the board than will result in the addition of two new members to the board in any twelve-month period; (b) director skills in policy development and in strategic issues of board choice.

B. *Authority:* no more than [*money amount*] and [*amount*] hours of management time, plus right to require all directors' attendance in training and development activities.

4. Compensation Committee

A. *Product:* annual CEO compensation package alternatives for board consideration, using any reasonable interpretation of the "CEO Compensation" policy. The package is to be presented for board consideration in such timely manner as to allow final affirmative action to be taken on the contract by both parties no later than [*amount*] days prior to the expiration of the term of the current CEO employment contract.

B. *Authority:* no more than [*money amount*], to include compensation surveys and outside counsel to draft contract, and use of no more than [*number*] hours of management time.

Policy 1.11: Cost Of Governance

Policy Category: Governance Process

The board will consciously invest in its ability to govern competently and wisely.

1. Board skills, methods, and supports will be sufficient to ensure governing with excellence.
    A. Training and retraining will be used liberally to orient new members and candidates for membership and to maintain and increase existing member skills and understandings.
    B. Outside monitoring assistance will be arranged so that the board can exercise confident control over organizational performance. This includes, but is not limited to, fiscal audit.
2. Costs will be prudently incurred, though not at the expense of endangering the development and maintenance of superior capability.
    A. Costs of external audits will be no more than [money amount] in [year], with [percentage] increases through [year].
    B. Costs of new director training and orientation will be no more than [money amount] per year in [year], with [percentage] increases through [year].
    C. Costs of board training, market analyses, futurists projections, and shareholder surveys will be no more than [money amount] in [year], with [percentage] increases through [year].

Policy 2.0: Delegation to the CEO

Policy Category: Board-Management Delegation

The board's sole official connection to the operational company, its achievements and its conduct, will be through a chief executive officer (CEO).

1. **Unity of Control.** Only officially passed motions of the board, speaking authoritatively as a group, are binding on the CEO.

2. **Accountability of the CEO.** The CEO is the board's only official link to operational achievement and conduct, so that all authority and accountability of management is considered by the board to be the authority and accountability of the CEO.

3. **Nature of CEO Delegation.** The board will instruct the CEO through written policies that prescribe the shareholder benefit to be achieved and describe organizational situations and actions to be avoided, allowing the CEO any reasonable interpretation of these policies.

4. **Monitoring CEO Performance.** Systematic and rigorous monitoring of CEO job performance will be solely against the provisions of the board's Ends policies and the board's Management Limitations policies.

5. **CEO Compensation.** CEO compensation will be decided by the board as a body and based on company performance and executive market conditions.

6. **CEO Termination.** CEO termination is an authority retained by the board, not delegated to any officer or committee.

Policy 2.1: Unity of Control

Policy Category: Board-Management Delegation

Only officially passed motions of the board, speaking authoritatively as a group, are binding on the CEO.

1. Decisions or instructions of individual directors, officers, or committees are not binding on the CEO except in rare instances when the board has specifically authorized such exercise of authority.

2. In the case of directors or committees requesting information or assistance without board authorization, the CEO can refuse such requests that require, in the CEO's opinion, a material amount of management time or funds or that are disruptive.

Policy 2.2: Accountability of the CEO

Policy Category: Board-Management Delegation

The CEO is the board's only official link to operational achievement and conduct, so that all authority and accountability of management is considered by the board to be the authority and accountability of the CEO.

1. The board will never give instructions to persons who report directly or indirectly to the CEO.
2. The board will not evaluate, either formally or informally, the job performance of any management position other than the CEO.
3. The board will view CEO performance as identical to total management performance, so that organizational accomplishment of board-stated Ends and avoidance of board-stated Management Limitations will be viewed as successful CEO performance. No performance measure established by the board or by organs of the board (such as a compensation committee) shall conflict with or modify this measure of performance.
4. All Management Limitations imposed on the CEO are limitations imposed on all management, so that violation by any part of the company is a violation by the CEO.

Policy 2.3: Nature of CEO Delegation

Policy Category: Board-Management Delegation

The board will instruct the CEO through written policies that prescribe the shareholder benefit to be achieved and describe organizational situations and actions to be avoided, allowing the CEO any reasonable interpretation of these policies.

1. The board will develop policies instructing that the company achieve certain benefits to shareholders. These policies will be developed systematically from the broadest, most general level to more defined levels, and will be called Ends policies.

2. The board will develop policies that limit the latitude the CEO may exercise in choosing the organizational methods, practices, conduct, and other means to achieving and protecting shareholder values. These policies will be developed systematically from the broadest, most general level to more defined levels, and they will be called Management Limitations policies.

3. As long as the CEO uses *any reasonable interpretation* of the board's Ends and Management Limitations policies, the CEO is authorized to establish all further policies, make all decisions, take all actions, establish all practices, and develop all activities.

4. The board may change its Ends and Management Limitations policies, thereby shifting the boundary between board and CEO domains. By doing so, the board changes the latitude of choice given to the CEO. But as long as any particular delegation is in place, the board will respect and support the CEO's choices.

Policy 2.4: Monitoring CEO Performance

Policy Category: Board-Management Delegation

Systematic and rigorous monitoring of CEO job performance will be solely against the provisions of the board's Ends policies and the board's Management Limitations policies.

1. Monitoring is simply to determine the degree to which board policies are being met. Data that do not do this will not be considered monitoring data.

2. The board will acquire monitoring data by one or more of three methods: (a) by internal report, in which the CEO discloses compliance information to the board; (b) by external report, in which an external, disinterested third party selected by the board assesses compliance with board policies; and (c) by direct board inspection, in which one or more designated members of the board assess compliance with the appropriate policy criteria.

3. In every case, the standard for compliance shall be *any reasonable CEO interpretation* of the board policy being monitored. The

board is the final arbiter of reasonableness but will always judge with a "reasonable person" test rather than with interpretations favored by individual directors or by the board as a whole.

4. All policies that instruct the CEO will be monitored at a frequency and by a method chosen by the board. The board can monitor any policy at any time by any method, but will ordinarily depend on a routine schedule.

POLICY	METHOD	FREQUENCY
Ends		
Shareholder Value	Internal (CEO)	Annually
Management Limitations		
Basic Executive Constraints	External (various)	Annually
Treatment of Stakeholders	Internal (CEO)	Annually
Treatment of Employees	Internal (CEO)	Annually
Financial Planning and Budgeting	Internal (CEO)	Quarterly
Financial Condition and Activities	Internal (CEO) External (Auditor)	Quarterly Annually
Asset Protection	External (Auditor)	Annually
Short-Term CEO Succession	Direct inspection (Chair)	Annually
Investments	External (Auditor)	Semiannually
Compensation and Benefits	Internal (CEO)	Annually
Trading in Company Securities	Internal (CEO)	Semiannually
Communication and Support	Direct inspection (Chair)	Annually
Diversification	Internal (CEO)	Semiannually

5. Periodic evaluation of the CEO and the evaluation-based component of any CEO compensation decision by the board will be

based on performance as demonstrated by the monitoring system described in this policy.

Policy 2.5: CEO Compensation

Policy Category: Board-Management Delegation

CEO compensation will be decided by the board as a body and based on company performance and executive market conditions.

1. Company performance will be only that performance revealed by the monitoring system to be directly related to criteria given by the board in policy.
2. Compensation will cover the entire range of salary, benefits, stock, and all other forms.
3. Compensation is to be competitive with similar performance within the marketplace while placing a substantial portion of the CEO's compensation at risk by tying it to Ends achievement and compliance with Management Limitations policies. The executive marketplace to be considered is companies of comparable size, challenges, and complexities.
4. A committee process will be used to gather information and to provide options and their implications to the full board for its decision.

Policy 2.6: CEO Termination

Policy Category: Board-Management Delegation

CEO termination is an authority retained by the board, not delegated to any officer or committee.

1. The decision process will be informed by performance data drawn from the monitoring system, which is itself directly related to CEO performance on criteria the board has stated in policy.
2. The board may choose to terminate for other reasons, but must then negotiate the terms of that termination or follow whatever provisions have been made by contract.

3. A committee process will be used to gather information and to provide options and their implications to the full board.

Policy 3.0: Shareholder Value
Policy Category: Ends

The ultimate aim of the company is return on shareholder equity better than the return for firms of similar risk characteristics.

1. Risk characteristics for comparison will include similar size, industry, and maturity of market.
2. Better return will mean above the median of such firms, rather than above the average.

[*Note:* For most publicly traded companies in North America, monetary shareholder value is the solitary reason for existence. For boards that take that position, a policy like this might work. Ends policies force boards to take a stand and define their terms. For example, other performance expectations that might have been chosen are that return on investment be greater than the cost of capital (perhaps with a further definition that the return is figured on a rolling three-year average rather than year by year) or that profitability be at least at the 80th percentile of profitability of companies in the same industry. Selecting among the possible meanings of shareholder value, given that shareholders themselves do not agree, is a sufficiently strategic contribution in itself to justify the existence of a board of directors.]

Policy 3.0: Shareholder Value
Policy Category: Ends

The company shall achieve _____% compounded growth in annual earnings per share by [*year*] and thereafter.

1. By the end of [*that year minus 3*] performance will be at least _____%.

2. By the end of [*that year minus 1*] performance will be at least
   _____%.

[*Note*: This too is a policy for a publicly traded company, though the board's approach would not be acceptable in all situations. This board chooses to hold the CEO accountable for growth in earnings per share, making the assumption that if the company performs successfully in these terms, the market will recognize and reward the success.]

Policy 3.0: Company Purpose

Policy Category: Ends

My company exists for my professional image and success.

1. A major impact in [*field of endeavor*] will be accomplished before 2015, with a reputation for fair play, competence, and integrity.
   A. The impact will be international in scope, but with emphasis on Australia and New Zealand.
   B. The amount of impact will, at least, be broad name identification, along with wide recognition that my ideas have caused substantial change in the practices of the field.
2. Sufficient funds earned by age fifty-five to enable comfortable retirement.

[*Note*: This Ends language was gleaned from a person with a wholly-owned corporation. Although making an agreed-on Ends statement is not as important for one person as it is for multiple directors, this sample shows that every company exists for specifiable ends, whether large or small. Further, having *image* as an end is legitimate only because it is an owner value. For a widely traded company, any image to be achieved would be company image (not shareholder image) and therefore it would be a means issue, not an ends issue at all.]

Policy 3.0: Purpose of Our Company

Policy Category: Ends

The purpose of our company is that we have the opportunity to be autonomous, to work at what we choose, and in our own way.

1. Financial rewards based on our own effort and intelligence, not affected by large company politics.
2. Opportunity to work with a technology we love and are stimulated by.
3. Collegiality of working with enthusiastic, committed partners of our choice.
4. Opportunity to change the way private wide-area-network satellite networks are architected, engineered, and maintained in retail and industrial vertical markets.

[*Note:* The founders and sole shareholders of a start-up high-technology company make it clear in this policy that the most important factor in owning their own business is the freedom to do things their own way. That, not purely monetary value, is the shareholder value that justifies for them all the trouble and risk of having the company. If these founders decide in the future to go to the equity market for capital, diluting their ownership, it is virtually certain that the ends of this company will change accordingly.]

Policy 3.0: Center of Family Occupational Life

Policy Category: Ends

The overall aim of our company is shared family wealth and work.

1. Our first priority is that the family stay together with appropriate, satisfying, and rewarding work for every adult member who chooses to be in the company.
2. Our second priority is that the worth of the company, and therefore the worth of each family member's shares, grows at a rate reasonably comparable to indexed funds.

[*Note:* This policy captured for a family the reason that they own and are determined to continue owning their own company. Certainly they want a financial return, but they've put equal emphasis on family togetherness. If they decide to make a public offering, this will change. Because the board will have a moral (and with some possible exceptions, legal) obligation to all shareholders, not just the family, the corporate ends will have to be adjusted to accommodate the new shareholders' different values.]

Policy 4.0: Basic Executive Constraints

Policy Category: Management Limitations

The CEO shall not cause or allow any practice, activity, decision, or organizational circumstance that is unlawful, imprudent, or in violation of generally accepted business and professional ethics or generally accepted accounting principles.

Further, without limiting the scope of the foregoing by this enumeration:

1. **Treatment of Stakeholders.** With respect to interactions with business partners, regulators, vendors, the local community, and the environment, the CEO shall not cause or allow conditions, procedures, or decisions that are unsafe, undignified, or unnecessarily intrusive.
2. **Treatment of Employees.** With respect to the treatment of employees, the CEO may not cause or allow conditions that are unsafe, unfair, or undignified.
3. **Financial Planning and Budgeting.** Financial planning for any fiscal year or the remaining part of any fiscal year shall not risk fiscal jeopardy, fail to be derived from a multiyear plan, or fail to be consistent with the company performance under Ends policies and other Management Limitations policies.
4. **Financial Conditions and Activities.** With respect to actual, ongoing financial conditions and activities, the CEO shall not cause or allow the development of fiscal jeopardy, compromised

fiduciary responsibility, or material deviation from the board's Ends policies.

5. **Emergency Loss of CEO.** The CEO shall not fail to protect the company from loss of its CEO.

6. **Asset Protection.** The CEO shall not allow corporate assets to be unprotected, inadequately maintained, or unnecessarily risked.

7. **Investments.** The CEO shall not fail to invest excess corporate funds to maximize after-tax interest income but in so doing shall not risk loss of principal or maintenance of proper liquidity.

8. **Compensation and Benefits.** With respect to employment, compensation, and benefits of employees, consultants, and contract workers, the CEO shall not cause or allow short-term or long-term jeopardy to fiscal integrity or to company image.

9. **Communication to and Support of the Board.** The CEO shall not permit the board to be uninformed or unsupported in its work.

10. **Trading in Company Securities.** The CEO shall not allow management personnel to trade in company securities under a less stringent code of integrity than the board has adopted for itself.

11. **Diversification.** The CEO shall not risk the company's future by failure to diversify.

12. **Dealings with Shareholders.** The CEO's relationship with shareholders shall neither violate the highest standards of transparency and responsiveness nor impede the board's role as shareholder representative.

Policy 4.1: Treatment of Stakeholders

Policy Category: Management Limitations

With respect to interactions with customers, business partners, regulators, vendors, the local community and the environment, the CEO shall not cause or allow conditions, procedures, or decisions that are unsafe, undignified, or unnecessarily intrusive.

Further, without limiting the scope of the foregoing by this enumeration, he or she shall not

1. Fail to operate facilities with appropriate environmental and community protection.
2. Fail to produce a safe, efficacious, and quality product when used in accordance with intended usage.
3. Fail to provide timely and consistent delivery of product.
4. Fail to comply with regulatory bodies governing the use and production of products and facility operations.

Policy 4.2: Treatment of Employees

Policy Category: Management Limitations

With respect to the treatment of employees, the CEO may not cause or allow conditions that are unsafe, unfair, or undignified.

Further, without limiting the scope of the foregoing by this enumeration, he or she shall not

1. Expose personnel to levels of occupational hazards greater than levels that are (a) below regulatory limits and (b) ALARA (as low as reasonably achievable).
2. Operate without written personnel rules that (a) clarify rules for employees, (b) provide for effective handling of grievances, and (c) protect against wrongful conditions, such as nepotism and grossly preferential treatment for personal reasons.
3. Discriminate against any employee for nondisruptive expression of dissent.
4. Fail to acquaint employees with the CEO's interpretation of their protections under this policy.

Policy 4.3: Financial Planning and Budgeting

Policy Category: Management Limitations

Financial planning for any fiscal year or the remaining part of any fiscal year shall not risk fiscal jeopardy, fail to be derived from a multiyear plan, or fail to be consistent with the company performance under Ends policies and other Management Limitations policies.

Further, without limiting the scope of the foregoing by this enumeration, the CEO shall not

1. Fail to include credible projection of revenues and expenses, separation of capital and operational items, cash flow, and disclosure of planning assumptions.
2. Plan expenditure in any fiscal year that would result in default under any of the corporation's financing agreements or cause the insolvency of the corporation.
3. Provide less for board prerogatives during the year than is set forth in the "Cost of Governance" policy.
4. Fail to plan so as to safeguard the company from unacceptable financial conditions enumerated in the "Financial Condition and Activities" policy.

Policy 4.4: Financial Condition and Activities

Policy Category: Management Limitations

With respect to actual, ongoing financial condition and activities, the CEO shall not cause or allow the development of fiscal jeopardy, compromised fiduciary responsibility, or material deviation from the board's Ends policies.

Further, without limiting the scope of the foregoing by this enumeration, he or she shall not

1. Maintain reserve accounts for the purposes of managing earnings to meet market expectations or for other questionable purposes.
2. Operate the company so as to cause it to be in default under any of its financial agreements.
3. Fail to follow [*applicable accounting standards*] in the maintenance of the financial records of the company.
4. Fail to settle payroll and debts in a timely manner.

5. Allow tax payments or other government-ordered payments or filings to be overdue or inaccurately filed.
6. Make a single purchase or commitment of greater than [*money amount*]. Splitting orders to avoid this limit is not acceptable.
7. Fail to aggressively pursue receivables after a reasonable grace period.

Policy 4.5: Emergency Loss of CEO

Policy Category: Management Limitations

The CEO shall not fail to protect the company from loss of its CEO.
   Further, without limiting the scope of the foregoing by this enumeration, he or she shall not

1. Have fewer than two other executives who are familiar with board and CEO issues and processes and who can provide emergency services.
2. Fail to have emergency short-term planning in place for this contingency.

Policy 4.6: Asset Protection

Policy Category: Management Limitations

The CEO shall not allow corporate assets to be unprotected, inadequately maintained, or unnecessarily risked.
   Further, without limiting the scope of the foregoing by this enumeration, he or she shall not

1. Fail to insure against theft and casualty losses to an appropriate level and against liability losses to directors, employees, and the organization itself in an amount greater than [*money amount*].
2. Fail to maintain adequate safeguards against any single employee's having access to material amounts of funds.
3. Subject plant and equipment to improper wear and tear or insufficient maintenance.

4. Unnecessarily expose the organization, its board, or its employees to claims of liability.
5. Make any purchase (a) wherein normally prudent protection has not been in place against conflict of interest, (b) of over [money amount] without having obtained comparative prices and quality, or (c) of over [money amount] without a stringent method of ensuring a balance of long-term quality and cost. Splitting orders to avoid these requirements is not allowed.
6. Undermine, cause to lose credibility, or otherwise jeopardize the independence and transparency of any relationship the board establishes with auditors or other entities of governance support.
    A. Purchase consulting service from either (a) the current audit firm or (b) a previous audit firm within three years of termination of its service.
    B. Retain as consultant or hire as employee any person who has been in the employ of the current or previous audit firm within the previous three years.
7. Fail to maintain adequate records storage, protecting intellectual property, information, and files from loss or significant damage.
8. Receive, process or disburse funds under controls that are insufficient to meet the board-appointed auditor's standards.
9. Fail to keep all appropriate licenses current.
10. Endanger the organization's public image or credibility, particularly in ways that would imperil achievement of Ends policies.
11. Fail to provide exceptional precautions against loss, damage, or deterioration of raw materials.

Policy 4.7: Investments

Policy Category: Management Limitations

The CEO shall not fail to invest excess corporate funds to maximize after-tax interest income but in so doing shall not risk loss in principal or maintenance of proper liquidity.

Policy 4.8: Compensation and Benefits

Policy Category: Management Limitations

With respect to the employment, compensation, and benefits of employees, consultants, and contract workers, the CEO shall not cause or allow short-term or long-term jeopardy to fiscal integrity or to company image.

Further, without limiting the scope of the foregoing by this enumeration, he or she shall not

1. Change his or her own compensation and benefits, except as his or her benefits are consistent with a package for all other employees.
2. Promise or imply permanent or guaranteed employment.
3. Establish current compensation and benefits that deviate materially from the geographical or professional market for the skills employed.
4. Create obligations over a longer term than revenues can be safely projected, in no event entering into agreements to promote and keep valuable employees for longer than five years.
5. Establish or change pension benefits so as to cause unpredictable or inequitable situations, including those that
   A. Incur unfunded liabilities that would put the company in jeopardy.
   B. Provide less than some basic level of benefits to all full-time employees.
   C. Allow any employee to lose benefits already accrued from any foregoing plan.
   D. Treat the CEO differently from other key employees.

Policy 4.9: Communication to and Support of the Board

Policy Category: Management Limitations

The CEO shall not permit the board to be uninformed or unsupported in its work.

Further, without limiting the scope of the foregoing by this enumeration, he or she shall not

1. Neglect to submit monitoring data required by the board in a timely, accurate, and understandable manner (see the "Monitoring CEO Performance" policy), directly addressing the provisions of the board policies being monitored.
2. Fail to report in a timely manner an actual or anticipated noncompliance with any board policy.
3. Let the board be unaware of relevant trends, anticipated adverse media coverage, threatened or pending lawsuits, backgrounds of all key management personnel, significant issues with major business partners, and material external and internal changes, particularly changes in the assumptions on which any board policy has previously been established.
4. Fail to advise the board if, in the CEO's opinion, the board is not in compliance with its own policies on Governance Process and Board-Management Delegation, particularly in the case of board behavior detrimental to the relationship between the board and the CEO.
5. Fail to marshal for the board as many management and external points of view, issues, and options as the board determines it needs for fully informed board choices.
6. Present information in an unnecessarily complex or lengthy form or in a form that fails to differentiate among information of three types: monitoring, decision preparation, and other.
7. Fail to provide a mechanism for board and committee meetings; for official board, officer, or committee communications; for maintenance of accurate board and director records; and for board disclosures required by law or deemed appropriate by the board.
8. Selectively disclose corporate information to individual directors or investors, with the exception of responding to officers or committees duly charged by the board.
9. Fail to supply the CEO's decisions along with applicable monitoring data for the board's consent agenda in respect to decisions

delegated to the CEO yet required by law or contract to be board approved.

Policy 4.10: Trading in Company Securities

Policy Category: Management Limitations

The CEO shall not allow management personnel to trade in company securities with a less stringent code of integrity than the board has adopted for itself.

Further, without limiting the scope of the foregoing by this enumeration, he or she shall not

1. Apply this proscription to fewer personnel than those at the level of vice president and directors of units with major relationships to accounting, finance, investment, or investor relations.

Policy 4.11: Diversification

Policy Category: Management Limitations

The CEO shall not risk the company's future by failure to diversify.

Further, without limiting the scope of the foregoing by this enumeration, he or she shall not

1. Fail to diversify beyond a single market or product so that if competitive market or general environmental factors affect that product or market, the viability of the company will not be threatened or severely damaged.
2. Fail to find new markets for existing products or new products, acquisitions, mergers, and innovative technologies sufficient that the resultant new products or markets will contribute at least [percentage] of earnings per share by [year].
3. Fail to be aware of any developing competitive threats and to plan for responding to them.

Policy 4.12: Dealings with Shareholders

Policy Category: Management Limitations

The CEO's relationship with shareholders will neither violate the highest standards of transparency nor impede the board's role as shareholder representative.

1. Information to shareholders, analysts, regulators, or other third parties will never obfuscate, cloud, be untimely, or otherwise obscure or misrepresent the company and its operations.

   A. GAAP will be interpreted conservatively in recording assets, liabilities, revenues, and earnings.

2. Management will take no actions and establish no relationships that interfere with the board as the primary link to shareholders or with the board's ability to provide appropriate oversight.

   A. Communications with shareholders shall not portray management as shareholders' ownership connection with the company.

   B. Relationships with auditors shall not involve significant management consulting contracts, making it imprudent for the shareholders to rely on the independence of those auditors.

Appendix F

Sample Monitoring Report Under Policy Governance

In the Policy Governance model, *monitoring* is the disclosure of data against criteria the board has enunciated in its policy language. The example in this appendix concerns monitoring CEO achievement of Ends and Management Limitations policies.[1] Whether the board grants a large or small amount of interpretive leeway in these policies, it demands that the CEO interpret as a reasonable person would. Therefore, a monitoring report must demonstrate that the CEO made a credible interpretation of the board's words and that this interpretation was in fact achieved. It is critical to the proper functioning of the monitoring system that the board count as acceptable *any reasonable interpretation*, not the interpretation the board had in mind but failed to say and not the after-the-fact opinion of individual directors.

Routine monitoring reports like the one shown here occur at a frequency and by a method determined by the board so that the monitoring process can follow a routine schedule (see the "Monitoring CEO Performance" policy in Appendix E).

In this example, the CEO is reporting company performance with respect to the board's Asset Protection policy, a Management Limitations policy. The CEO states where his or her interpretation has not changed since the last report, making it possible for directors to read through more quickly. Where board policy has not been successfully implemented, the CEO's notation clearly shows that failure. Also in this example, the CEO makes the case that the broadest statement (the preamble of the board's policy) is completely monitored by the monitoring of the subordinate parts.

Unless the board finds this argument to be reasonable, the global statement must be specifically monitored as well.

Internal Monitoring Report
Asset Protection
January 2010

I hereby present my monitoring report on your Executive Limitations policy "Asset Protection" according to the schedule set out. I certify that the information contained in this report is true.

Signed _____, CEO

Date   _____

BROADEST POLICY PROVISION

The CEO shall not allow the assets to be unprotected, inadequately maintained, or unnecessarily risked.

CEO's Interpretation

[NO CHANGE SINCE LAST REPORT] I submit that the board has comprehensively interpreted this policy in its subsequent policy provisions. My interpretations and data will be attached to those provisions, below.

POLICY PROVISION 1

The CEO shall not fail to insure against theft and casualty losses to at least 80% replacement value and against liability losses to board members, staff, and the organization itself in an amount greater than the average for comparable organizations.

CEO's Interpretation

[NO CHANGE SINCE LAST REPORT] Insurance against theft and casualty losses is unjustified if the cost of insurance is higher than the cost of the potential loss. Accordingly, I have interpreted this aspect of the policy to mean that physical assets over $2,000 in value must be insured. This threshold has been established in consultation with two insurance professionals, neither of whom are currently supplying this organization with insurance. Full replacement value is prudent on high-value assets such as buildings and vehicles. Other equipment used in this organization, being of lesser value, can be insured at 80% to 90% replacement value. The lower cost of insurance at this level would permit a cost saving that offsets the potential cost of funding part of possible future losses.

Liability insurance in our field is commonly obtained in an amount of $2m, according to the National Association of Organizations Like Ours (NAOLO). Significantly greater coverage, up to $2.5m, can be obtained with only marginal increased costs.

Data

Review of our fixed asset inventory demonstrates that all assets above $2,000 in value are covered by insurance. Additions to this inventory that are purchased periodically must have insurance coverage in place prior to delivery and installation. A check made of items purchased in the last six months shows that with one exception, this requirement has been met. The exception was due to a delivery made in advance of schedule.

Liability insurance coverage, provided by the XXX Insurance Co., Inc, is in place for board members, staff, and the organization itself, and is in the amount of $2.5m.

I report compliance.

POLICY PROVISION 2

The CEO shall not allow unbonded personnel access to material amounts of funds.

CEO's Interpretation

[ITALIZED SECTION CHANGED SINCE LAST REPORT]
"Unbonded personnel" is interpreted to mean employees who are

refused inclusion in the organization's insurance against employee wrongdoing. "Material" is interpreted to mean any amount over $500 per access *or $5,000 cumulatively in a twelve-month period*. This interpretation was based on advice received from the organization's auditor as well as from NAOLO. Personnel who have "access" is interpreted to mean those who, due to the course of their duties, should be included in the insurance against employee wrongdoing. "Funds" means not only the amounts mentioned above but also items convertible to funds, including the organization's checks, check signing machine, petty cash, and purchase order forms.

Data

A review of our insurance covering employee wrongdoing shows that all employees who have access as defined are listed. Procedures are in place that protect access to petty cash, checks, signing machines, and purchase order forms. A spot check conducted in the last week demonstrated that in all cases, no access can be obtained by unauthorized persons, and that no access is possible without the knowledge of two key holders.

I report compliance.

POLICY PROVISION 3

The CEO shall not subject plant and equipment to improper wear and tear or insufficient maintenance.

CEO's Interpretation

[ITALIZED SECTION CHANGED SINCE LAST REPORT] "Improper wear and tear" is interpreted to be use for which the item was not designed, and use by persons not trained in the proper treatment of the asset. "Insufficient maintenance" is interpreted to be a preventive maintenance schedule that is not in compliance with manufacturer-recommended guidelines, or lack of adherence to a proper schedule. "Plant and equipment" is interpreted to be buildings, machinery (industrial and office), vehicles, and grounds. *Plant and equipment scheduled to be replaced in the next twelve-month period is excluded from this definition.*

Data

Ongoing preventive maintenance for qualified assets is provided either by maintenance contract or directly by our in-house mechanics. Unseasonable wet weather has prevented the completion of scheduled maintenance on outdoor loading dock equipment. This deficiency is expected to be righted in the next month. With the exception of forklift racing that was discovered to be going on in the shipping department, no undue wear and tear on equipment is reported. However, undue wear and tear on plant is reported in the case of the warehouse, currently unused by us, that the Hooligan Children's Club was allowed to use for its summer party. Although we remain committed to participating and contributing to community life, it is clear that we need to be more selective and to provide better supervision of those with whom we share our assets. A review last month of personnel records shows documentation that all operators of equipment have been trained in proper use of that equipment.

I REPORT **VIOLATION** OF THIS POLICY.

POLICY PROVISION 4

The CEO shall not unnecessarily expose the organization, its board, or staff to claims of liability.

CEO's Interpretation

[NO CHANGE SINCE LAST REPORT] Unnecessary exposure to claims of liability is interpreted to mean allowing risks to be taken that are not called for in the normal course of business. In our field the most prominent examples are in the area of safety. Although regulated by several government departments, all of which audit for compliance with their requirements, our organization must pay special attention to the safety of the public who visit in the role of customers or advocates. The NAOLO has a publication that outlines prudent safeguards against injury to such persons. It is my interpretation that because these safeguards are the most comprehensive available, they must be adopted and followed in our organization.

Data

We were audited by all relevant government departments since the last monitoring report was presented, and we passed in every case. NAOLO reviewed our compliance with its recommended guidelines and found us to be in equally complete compliance.

I report compliance.

POLICY PROVISION 5

The CEO shall not make any purchase (a) wherein normally prudent protection has not been given against conflict of interest, (2) of over $2,000 without having obtained comparative prices and quality, or (c) of over $200,000 without a stringent method of ensuring the balance of long-term quality and cost.

CEO's Interpretation

[ITALIZED SECTION CHANGED SINCE LAST REPORT] "Conflict of interest" is defined as allowing purchasing decisions to be made on the basis of improper preference. Preference for a vendor who is a relative or close associate is prohibited, and protection against such a basis for purchasing decisions is the requirement for disclosure of such interests, as well as the requirement for two signatories on purchase orders. Purchases of over $2,000 require comparison pricing of at least three options. Comparisons need to be noted. *The lowest price need not be chosen.* Exceptions are made when there are no or few options and when the purchase is a recurring one (in which case, comparisons must be obtained on an annual basis). "A stringent method" of ensuring the balance of long-term quality and cost is in our field almost always an RFP process. The lowest price need not be chosen.

Data

Our auditor was asked to randomly review purchases made in the last six months to monitor compliance with my interpretations of your policy. One hundred purchases were reviewed. Although there were purchases where no note was made of comparison shopping, compliance was reported at the 96% level.

I report compliance.

POLICY PROVISION 6

The CEO shall not fail to protect intellectual property, information, and files from loss or significant damage.

CEO's Interpretation

[NO CHANGE SINCE LAST REPORT] "Intellectual property" is interpreted to mean our property as well as that of others. Our intellectual property is our industrial process and formulas and our customized software. We use significant amounts of the intellectual property of others, including software and systems that are trademarked as the property of others. The property of others may not be bootlegged or used without attribution. Our own intellectual property is trademarked or patented, and a search service is employed to monitor its unauthorized use. Unauthorized users must be prosecuted. "Information and files" are those referring to personnel, finances, customers, ordering, maintenance, marketing, and the myriad other pursuits of the organization. Loss or damage that results from computer problems such as viruses, hacking, or system failure must be prevented. Losses or damage due to fire, flood, or theft must also be prevented. I interpret appropriate safeguards to be those normally pursued by prudent businesses, for example, very frequent backups, off-site storage of information, fireproof storage, virus protection, and firewalls.

Data

There are no bootlegged software programs used in our organization according to a random check carried out two weeks ago. Attribution of the intellectual property of others is not systematic and needs improvement. We are currently pursuing two other organizations that are using our trademarked materials without authorization. All protections noted as my interpretations are in place, and a survey of adherence to these requirements shows that they are observed and continually updated.

I report compliance.

POLICY PROVISION 7

The CEO shall not receive, process, or disburse funds under controls that are insufficient to meet the board-appointed auditor's standards.

CEO's Interpretation

[NO CHANGE SINCE LAST REPORT] The board-appointed auditor's standards are GAAP. The auditor also makes suggestions in the management letter. I interpret these suggestions to become standards once management has accepted the suggestions.

Data

Your last audit received an unqualified report from your auditors. Management has found several of the suggestions in the management letter to be very helpful and will complete their full implementation by two months from the date of this report.

I report compliance.

Notes

Introduction

1. J. K. Louden, *The Effective Director in Action* (New York: AMA-COM, 1975), p. 117.

Chapter One

1. D.S.R. Leighton and D. H. Thain, *Making Boards Work: What Directors Must Do to Make Canadian Boards Effective* (Whitby, Ont.: McGraw-Hill Ryerson, 1997), p. 26.
2. J. A. Conger, E. E. Lawler III, and D. L. Finegold, *Corporate Boards: New Strategies for Adding Value at the Top* (San Francisco: Jossey-Bass, 2001); D. L. Finegold, E. E. Lawler III, and J. A. Conger, "To Whom Are Boards Accountable?" *The Corporate Board*, 2001, 22(129), 17–22.
3. The process and advisability of appealing to different investors is given thorough treatment by C. K. Brancato, *Institutional Investors and Corporate Governance: Best Practices for Increasing Corporate Value* (Chicago: Irwin, 1997).

Chapter Two

1. A. Demb and F.-F. Neubauer, *The Corporate Board: Confronting the Paradoxes* (New York: Oxford University Press, 1992), p. 1.
2. This use of *for* and *does* to refer to concepts that are similar to the Policy Governance definitions of *ends* and *means* was introduced

by John Argenti. We make frequent use of this handy verbal device and so are indebted to J. Argenti, *Your Organization: What Is It For?* (Berkshire, England: McGraw-Hill International, 1993).

Chapter Three

1. R. Charan, *Boards at Work: How Corporate Boards Create Competitive Advantage* (San Francisco: Jossey-Bass, 1998), p. xvii.
2. R. K. Greenleaf, *Trustees as Servants* (Indianapolis: Greenleaf Center for Servant-Leadership, 1991) and *Servant-Leadership: A Journey into the Nature of Legitimate Power and Greatness* (New York: Paulist Press, 1977).
3. J. Carver, *The Unique Double Servant-Leadership Role of the Board Chairperson*, Booklet No. 2, Voices of Servant-Leadership Series (Indianapolis: Greenleaf Center for Servant-Leadership, Feb. 1999).

Chapter Four

1. R. I. Tricker, "Corporate Governance—the Subject Whose Time Has Come," *Corporate Governance: An International Review*, 2000, 8(4), 289–296.

Chapter Five

1. A. Cadbury, *The Company Chairman*, 2nd ed. (Hemel Hempstead, U.K.: Director Books, 1995), p. 14.
2. R.A.G. Monks, "Shareholder Activism: A Reality Check," *The Corporate Board*, 2001, 22(129), 23–26.

Chapter Six

1. Sophocles, as quoted in T. Goodman (ed.), *The Forbes Book of Business Quotations* (New York: Black Dog and Leventhal, 1997), p. 498.

Chapter Seven

1. Organization for Economic Cooperation and Development, Preamble, OECD Principles of Corporate Governance (Paris: Organization for Economic Cooperation and Development, 1999).

Chapter Eight

1. Niccolò Machiavelli, The Prince, N. H. Thomson (trans.) (New York: Dover, 1992), p. 13. (Originally published 1910 by P. F. Collier & Son, New York.)
2. Currently, the only training that prepares consultants for Policy Governance to a standard recognized by John Carver, creator of the model, is the Policy Governance Academy[SM], operated by Carver Governance Design, Inc., Atlanta.
3. J. Carver, Boards That Make a Difference, 2nd ed. (San Francisco: Jossey-Bass, 1997); C. G. Royer, School Board Leadership 2000 (Houston: Brockton, 1996); J. Carver and M. M. Carver, Reinventing Your Board (San Francisco: Jossey-Bass, 1997); J. Carver, John Carver on Board Leadership (San Francisco: Jossey-Bass, 2002).
4. C. Oliver and others, The Policy Governance Fieldbook: Practical Lessons, Tips, and Tools from the Experiences of Real-World Boards (San Francisco: Jossey-Bass, 1999).
5. J. Carver, "The Opportunity for Reinventing Corporate Governance in Joint Venture Companies," Corporate Governance: An International Review, 2000, 8(1), 75–80.
6. J. Carver, "Families of Boards, Part Two: Holding Companies," in J. Carver, Board Leadership: A Bimonthly Workshop with John Carver, No. 27 (San Francisco: Jossey-Bass, 1996).
7. A. A. Berle Jr. and G. C. Means, The Modern Corporation and Private Property (New York: Commerce Clearing House, 1932).

Appendix B

1. J. G. Beaver, The Effective Board, cited in A. Cadbury, The Company Chairman, 2nd ed. (Hemel Hempstead, U.K.: Director

Books, 1995), p. 23; M. Lipton and J. Lorsch, "Dissenting and Concurring Views," in *The Will to Act,* Report of the Subcommittee on Corporate Governance and Financial Markets to the Competitiveness Policy Council, cited in W. G. Bowen, *Inside the Boardroom: Governance by Directors and Trustees* (New York: Wiley, 1994), p. 87; Heidrick and Struggles International, *The Role of Chairman,* cited in A. Cadbury, *The Company Chairman,* p. 23; R. Charan, *Boards at Work: How Corporate Boards Create Competitive Advantage* (San Francisco: Jossey-Bass, 1998).
2. Cadbury, *The Company Chairman,* p. 10.

Appendix C

1. G. Mills, cited in A. Cadbury, *The Company Chairman,* 2nd ed. (Hemel Hempstead, U.K.: Director Books, 1995), p. 9.
2. D.S.R. Leighton and D. H. Thain, *Making Boards Work: What Directors Must Do to Make Canadian Boards Effective* (Whitby, Ont.: McGraw-Hill Ryerson, 1997), pp. 44–45.
3. A. Cadbury, "The Corporate Governance Agenda," *Corporate Governance: An International Review,* 2000, 8(1), p. 10.
4. R. H. Carlsson, *Ownership and Value Creation: Strategic Corporate Governance in the New Economy* (New York: Wiley, 2001), p. 47.
5. J. W. Lorsch and E. MacIver, *Pawns or Potentates: The Reality of America's Corporate Boards* (Boston: Harvard Business School Press, 1989), pp. 94, 184.
6. K. N. Dayton, *Governance Is Governance* (Washington, D.C.: Independent Sector, 1987), pp. 7–8.
7. W. Knowlton and I. Millstein, "Can the Board of Directors Help the American Corporation Earn the Immortality It Holds So Dear?" in J. R. Meyer and J. M. Gustafson (eds.), *The U.S. Business Corporation: An Institution in Transition* (New York: Ballinger, 1988), pp. 169–191.
8. J. Whitehead, cited in W. G. Bowen, *Inside the Boardroom: Governance by Directors and Trustees* (New York: Wiley, 1994), p. 83.

9. D. J. Gogel, cited by Carlsson, *Ownership and Value Creation*, p. 49.

10. H. Williams, "Corporate Accountability and Corporate Power," in *Power and Accountability: The Changing Role of the Corporate Board*, Benjamin Farless Memorial Lectures (Pittsburgh: Carnegie-Mellon University Press, 1979), p. 18.

11. A. Patton and J. C. Baker, "Why Directors Won't Rock the Boat," *Harvard Business Review*, 1987, pp. 10–18.

12. Ipsos-Reid Corporation, "The View of the Boardroom," [www.angusreid.com/media], Oct. 30, 2001.

13. McKinsey & Company, "Investor Opinion Survey on Corporate Governance," [www.gcgf.org/docs/72CGBrochure.pdf], June 2000.

14. J. A. Conger, E. E. Lawler III, and D. L. Finegold, *Corporate Boards: New Strategies for Adding Value at the Top* (San Francisco: Jossey-Bass, 2001), p. 58.

15. R. H. Carlsson, *Ownership and Value Creation*, p. 70.

16. Cadbury, *The Company Chairman*, p. 13; Heidrick and Struggles International, *The Role of Chairman*, cited in Cadbury, *The Company Chairman*, p. 23.

17. R. Charan, *Boards at Work: How Corporate Boards Create Competitive Advantage* (San Francisco: Jossey-Bass, 1998), p. 50–51.

18. J. G. Beaver, *The Effective Board*, quoted in Cadbury, *The Company Chairman*, p. 23.

19. Although they do not argue for this point, it is discussed by M. Lipton and J. Lorsch, "Dissenting and Concurring Views," in *The Will to Act*, Report of the Subcommittee on Corporate Governance and Financial Markets to the Competitiveness Policy Council, quoted in Bowen, *Inside the Boardroom*, p. 87.

20. Charan, *Boards at Work*, p. 51 (emphasis in the original).

21. H. W. Jenkins Jr., "When CEOs Fail, Blame the Board," *Wall Street Journal*, Nov. 7, 2001, p. A23.

22. Heidrick and Struggles International, *The Role of Chairman*, cited in Cadbury, *The Company Chairman*, p. 23.

23. Although they do not argue for this point, it is discussed by Lipton and Lorsch, "Dissenting and Concurring Views," quoted in Bowen, *Inside the Boardroom*, p. 87.

24. Charan, *Boards at Work*, p. 51.
25. Cadbury, *The Company Chairman*, p. 13 (emphasis in the original).
26. Although they do not argue for this point, it is discussed by Lipton and Lorsch, "Dissenting and Concurring Views," cited in Bowen, *Inside the Boardroom*, p. 87.
27. Charan, *Boards at Work*, p. 51.
28. Charan, *Boards at Work*, pp. 50–51.
29. R. D. Ward, *21st Century Corporate Board* (New York: Wiley, 1997), p. 10ff, chronicles this event in detail.
30. Bowen, *Inside the Boardroom*, p. 87.

Appendix D

1. J. Balkcom and D. Tormey, "The Street Fight over Board-Management Polity," *The Corporate Board*, 1998, *19*(111), 11–16.
2. E. Sternberg, *Just Business: Business Ethics in Action* (Boston: Little, Brown, 1994); Balkcom and Tormey, "The Street Fight over Board-Management Polity"; J. W. Lorsch and E. MacIver, *Pawns or Potentates: The Reality of America's Corporate Boards* (Boston: Harvard Business School Press, 1989).

Appendix F

1. Our thanks to Miriam Carver for her preparation of this report.

Acknowledgments

Our greatest debt is to those thinkers and practitioners whose inquiring minds preceded us, persons too numerous to mention, not only in governance but also in management and even philosophy. Our clients and colleagues have also contributed enormously to perfecting ideas through practical application. Due to confidentiality agreements, we must appreciate these clients without specific citations, though their contributions of board policies and monitoring reports to be adapted for this text were invaluable. To the directors and CEOs who were so gracious, we say thanks.

Generously agreeing to comment on the manuscript in process were James Gillies, Schulich School of Business, York University, Toronto; Dana Hermanson, Cole School of Business, Kennesaw University, Kennesaw, Georgia; Rodney Insall, former vice president, Corporate Governance, BP-Amoco, London; and John Herndon, director, Christine Jacobs, CEO and chairman, and Bruce Smith, CFO, all with Theragenics Corporation, Duluth, Georgia. Miriam Carver, governance consultant and author (as well as wife of John), offered useful critiques of theory-practice consistency. Thanks are also due to others who offered advice from their experience of working in a variety of corporate environments, including Jonathan Huffman, Peter Cowern, Lance MacIntosh, and Ray Tooley. Ivan Benson of the Carvers' office kept the logistics in order. Susan Williams of Jossey-Bass, besides providing cordial editorial support, supplied the encouragement for writing this book in the first place.

We owe a particular debt to Adrian Cadbury for his graciousness in writing the Foreword. Sir Adrian's leadership in corporate governance is legend. His support and encouragement cannot be overvalued. Finally, we are delighted to acknowledge those readers willing to give a fair hearing to a new approach in the service of effective, prudent, ethical corporations.

J.C.
C.O.

The Authors

John Carver is the creator of what is widely considered the world's first (and still only) theory of governance. His redesign of the governing board task, constructed as a universally applicable paradigm, is already well noted in governmental and NGO fields and is being increasingly recognized for its applicability in business.

Carver holds a B.S. degree in business and economics (1965), an M.Ed. degree in educational psychology (1965) from the University of Tennessee at Chattanooga, and a Ph.D. degree in clinical psychology (1968) from Emory University, Atlanta. He became a member of the honorary scientific research society Sigma Xi in 1968. He served in the U.S. Air Force and as an officer of a small, family-owned manufacturing company before assuming three successive public management CEO positions.

Carver has testified before committees of state legislatures and the U.S. Congress. He has consulted on governance issues in North and South America, Europe, Africa, and Asia. He has worked with the governance of governmental and NGO organizations of up to $52 billion in assets and with the chief executive level of a national department of defense. Over the past decade he has also worked with corporate boards.

Carver is author of *Boards That Make a Difference* (1990, 1997), *John Carver on Board Leadership* (2002), *A New Vision of Board Leadership* (with Miriam Mayhew, 1994), *Reinventing Your Board* (with Miriam Mayhew Carver, 1997), and more than 150 journal articles. His fourteen published monographs include *The Unique Double Servant Leadership Role of the Board Chairperson* (1999) and

Business Leadership on Nonprofit Boards (1980). He has previously held positions as adjunct or visiting faculty at several institutions, and is currently adjunct professor at the Schulich School of Business, York University, Toronto and the University of Georgia Institute for Nonprofit Organizations, Athens. John Carver and Miriam Carver, his wife and governance consultant, live in Atlanta. Contact him at 404-728-9444 or johncarver@carvergovernance.com or visit his Web site at www.carvergovernance.com.

Caroline Oliver has worked with boards as a senior executive and director in Europe since the 1970s, in Canada, and the United States. She has also served on advisory committees to the U.K. government and the European Economic Community. She trained with John Carver in Atlanta in 1995. Curious about how his model of governance worked in practice, she brought together seven experts and eleven organizations to write *The Policy Governance Fieldbook: Practical Lessons, Tips and Tools from the Experience of Real-World Boards* (1998), which illustrated that although few boards come close to perfect practice, all the boards studied reported significant benefits. In 1999, Oliver co-organized an international think tank on the future of Policy Governance, which led to the formation of the International Policy Governance Association in June 2001, which she chairs. The association's aim is "high quality Policy Governance implementation" within the context of "owner accountable productive organizations."

As a governance consultant, Oliver works with a wide variety of boards and regularly contributes to *Board Leadership* journal. Oliver; her husband, Ian Burgess, candle entrepreneur; and their two children, Anna and Fiona, live in Oakville, Ontario. Contact her at 905-337-9412 or coliver@carolineoliver.com or visit her Web site at www.carolineoliver.com.

Index